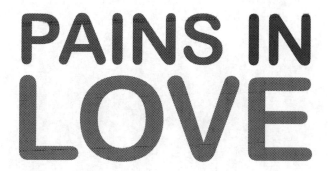

PAINS IN LOVE

Shola Azeez Oyeyinka

Order this book online at www.trafford.com
or email orders@trafford.com

Most Trafford titles are also available at major online book retailers.

Printed in the United States of America.

ISBN: 978-1-4907-2416-4 (sc)
ISBN: 978-1-4907-2417-1 (hc)
ISBN: 978-1-4907-2418-8 (e)

Library of Congress Control Number: 2014900671

Trafford rev. 03/05/2014

 www.trafford.com

North America & international
toll-free: 1 888 232 4444 (USA & Canada)
fax: 812 355 4082

This book is a true narration of events that happened along the corridor of the author's life. Names and places in this story have been omitted or changed to protect the privacy of the people involved. However, it proclaims the absolute reality of the event. *Love* can be interesting at a time of glory, but it is also a monster that kills in the darkest moment of time.

DEDICATION

To my son, Kareem Ayomide Oyeyinka, and in the memory of my late parents, Mr. and Mrs. S. O Oyeyinka. May their gentle souls rest in perfect peace of the Lord.

Acknowledgment

No effort can be accomplished without the assistance and co-operation from many along the way.

My everlasting thanks and honor go to God almighty, the supreme power of time, who despite every obstacle and tribulation along the way, never stopped inspiring my heart to a complete package of my intention.

I am indebted to my late parents who taught me self-confidence and self-reliance. People like them do not need to die at all, but who am I to challenge the wish of the most high, our Lord? My love for them will endure forever. Rest in peace, Dad and Mum.

My profound gratitude goes to many out there, who fought endlessly for this work not to be successful. It has never been their fault in anyway, for without them along the bridge of time, nothing can really be accomplished. They taught me awareness and relentlessness in what I believed in. Indeed, without them on the ladder of fate, life is no fun and has no meaning to write home about.

I express my divine appreciation to my beloved wife, Moronke Titilayo Oyeyinka, a woman of great understanding. She took it a challenge upon herself to see to the end product of this book. Her valuable suggestions all through were a shade of mountains that pushes me on. To my son Kareem Ayomide Oyeyinka, who never stopped wondering and asking what the hell I am writing every time.

My editor, pastor Elvis Iruh of the *Voice Magazine* Amsterdam. A man of great ideology. I thank him for all mechanism putting across to bring this labor to a realization.

I thank my technical adviser, Mr. Ladi N. Okanlawon, for all his motivation when my tears gushed into the sea. He was there for me when others walked away and when I needed a friend to talk to.

I thank Joel Berou, my publishing consultant, Trafford publishing, and Earl Thomas, check-in coordinator, for their concern and professionalism on this work.

To all my well wishers who contributed in one way or the other toward getting it done, a package of goodies to you all.

Finally, I wish to recognize the effort of many out there in the public world who are working very hard to achieve a goal in life; I wish everyone every success in whatever they hope to achieve.

S. A Oyeyinka

INTRODUCTION

"You can do better than this," Papa said. "Where is that knowledge of literature I used to see in you?" "But, Papa, I gave you the introduction I wrote yesterday. What do you think of it?" "Not good enough. You can do better than that, not after such experience as you have had. Get another piece of paper and write something more meaningful. The world out there is anxiously waiting to read your story." He pointed his hand in the air with that half-annoyed look on his face. I looked at him and smile. "I wonder what I would've done in life without you, Papa," I said in admiration. "You are one in a million fathers," I said to him the way I felt within.

Having received the inspiration from my father, I rolled out in my wheelchair into the garden with a pen and a notebook in my hand to write, to challenge my memory, and to see how best I could recall past events in my life.

I don't want to fall victim anymore to such despicable ignorance of my past.

To the best of what I can remember, Papa said I was in coma for five months. Despite the struggles they had to go through, they watched over me and saw me recover and come back to life. They never gave up on me. They never gave up their usual belief in God, that He is the owner of life and that He heals all pains. Though I lost some of my memory during my recovery and my legs are still not functioning properly as expected, at least I am alive, full of hope for a better future. That is what matters now. Above all, I have my parents whose body and soul live inside of me till eternity, and they love me too.

We no longer live in my village, Iyatan. Papa is now one of the chief judges of the Supreme Court of Nigeria, so we moved to a more exclusive area at spring close in Ikoyi Lagos.

I love to write most importantly about life in general and particularly about challenging the memories of my past. I can still remember my younger sister, Moji. Although I don't vividly remember our childhood life together, I was told she now lives in the United Kingdom where she is studying Law at Al burn Law College. Mama told me that we were very fond of each other and we played together. Such a bond of unity and love we shared for each other. My parents thought we would never be separated from each other, but we had to find our purpose in life as we moved toward our destiny, and for that reason, she moved abroad for further studies.

My intention of writing this book is not to praise what my parents told me or not for the sake of writing. My motivation is to use my story to teach some lessons so other innocent people do not repeat my mistakes in life as my story will recount. To fully regain my memory would take time. I think patience on my part will do me a lot of good as I continue the exercise of tasking myself to remember all I can. I do that often by just sitting at the garden and playing with my thoughts, which has helped me to regain a lot of lost memories now, and the experience is amazing.

Mama walked into the garden and found me lost in my ocean of mind. She had been standing behind me for sometime without me noticing her. I didn't just notice that she was there. "Oh, Mama, you are here!" I said.

"Yes," she replied. "I have been trying to improve my knowledge of literature," I said and smiled. It was a stressful smile though, but what else can I do. She said nothing. I observed some tears gently rolling down her face. She wiped them away as quickly as possible.

"God bless you, my son, Paul. What happened to you was never your fault." She came and stood before me and placed her right hand on my right shoulder. "With the authority of a mother, I pray for you and bless you with my utmost blessings to be successful in life and to be one among the righteous in the hereafter. Come in, my son, for your lunch is ready." She rolled me into the house while still crying gently.

Papa would not appreciate that, and she knows it. Hence, she quickly began to clean her face with her wrapper. Papa was hungry; he is such an extrovert when it comes to talking about his stomach. He never jokes with that, not even for his enemy. He came out of his study room to join us on the dinning table. "Let me see what you have there," he said, and he collected it from me.

He focused closely on it and began to nod his head. "This is more like it, son. Clear your mind, and drive your message home in your story. You can do it, my son. I know you can. I also know that someday you will walk on your two feet again and you shall become the hero everyone has wanted to see in you. That should be your desire, son, a test of your faith in God almighty."

CHAPTER ONE

I have never written a story before, never had the know-how. Sometimes I am just kind of paranoid when I think of how to begin with one sentence or express my feelings in the best way possible so that it would hit the target in such a way that would make people around me to understand my inward feelings and share my emotions.

I have always wanted to write my story for years now, but I just simply could not hem back on it. I don't know why. It maybe because of the shock I'd received from the incident, or maybe I was not just bold enough to write my experience that one way or the other would've stood as a nightmare throughout my entire lifetime. Whichever way it proved to be, my father would not allow me to submit to the trick of the devil that was trying to deny me the pleasure of writing my story. I am grateful on his verdict to get me off my shell as a great fulfillment any parent would have to help children they love so much.

I and my immediately younger sister Moji were the best fulfillment our parents ever cherished in their life. At that time, I was twenty-one years old, while Moji was nineteen, two years younger than me. Our parents cared a lot about us. I used this expression because I know how much they love us and how much they gave us the gift of life. Somehow we were just a close family that made a perfect team, and we love it since it makes us understand each other's feelings to a greater extent and the people around us.

Papa works as a lawyer and is now living in the big city of Lagos, but we remain in the smaller home town of Iyatan. He usually comes home every week to visit us. He never misses a weekend with his family. However, some weekends, he cannot make it because of his busy work. Iyatan is not that far from Lagos; it takes about two hours with a speed limit of eighty kilometers per hour to reach Iyatan from Lagos.

Mama is a professional trader. She sells beer and other small things like provisions for household use. In fact, she is a wholesale distributor of the Nigeria Breweries in Lagos. This gave us the honor of being known among the villagers, as the children of prominent parents.

Moji and I attended the same school in Iyatan. St. Jones High school was a popular school that bears lots of merits to its credit. Apart from being a government school, its recognition by the West African Examination Council (WAEC) made it worth being listed on a front-role recognition among all other schools in my town and around Lagos.

Mama didn't had enough time to convey us to school every morning and bring us back home, so we often commuted by the school bus throughout our years at St. Jones. However, it wasn't the same with other schools in Iyatan. There was no such transportation arrangement for other students; most of them walked to school. St. Jones high school was special for its well-organized structure, and it was convenient for parents to have their children there.

As usual, at closing time, Mike Onubi, my best friend, and I sat on one of the front row seats behind the driver, and discussing the next football competition that was going to take place between St. Jones high school and Pitterlock College. My interest on the subject was very deep that I did not notice for how long Mike had been pinching my legs beneath to get my attention to notice a girl sitting just directly opposite us and gazing languorously at us.

"Are you out of your mind?" he whispered slowly in my ear.

"What is it?" I questioned eagerly. "That girl." He gestured with his little finger. "You won't believe how much she has been looking at you, especially since we sat here. Do you know her from somewhere?" he questioned.

"No, of course not." I glanced in her direction to see if she was still looking at us. I guess she sensed that we were talking about her. She had changed her posture to look outside the window.

"Ooh,ooh! What a nice girl she appears to look!" Mike whispered in the same low tone as mine.

"Check her uniform, stainless as compared to other girls in the school." "You know what," I said, "my instinct tells me she's up to something." He laughed.

"You may be right. Girls these days are full of pretense. Sometimes, they make it hard to predict. Anyway, it's all a matter of love. After all, that's what the world is all about."

"Am sure you don't want my company in such a relationship," I replied.

He blinked and looked somewhat offended. "I've told you, best friend, never be too far from the real world. You are not going to be an antisocial kind of person, would you?"

"Well," I answered stubbornly, "you know me already. There is no reason to go over all this again." "Okay," he said, adjusting his position in his seat, "the purpose of friendship is to enlighten one another about life."

As he was speaking, I had a hunch. My instinct made me raise my head again. I did. Maybe I should say she was unlucky this time. My eyes caught her looking closely at me with an open indication of insight that speaks too well of its meaning. I knew such a look when I see one. What I saw in her was deep interest in something, but I was not sure what.

A glimmer of smile drop on her face as she noticed me looking at her.I began to feel somewhat dominated by her strange, direct look. Something unknown began to influence my inner self. And as a result, I was becoming uncomfortable toward the whole development.

"Hey," Mike uttered at once, bringing my thoughts back to life. "I left my biology text book with John. I would need it at home tonight. I better go for it now."

"It's okay. I have two of them here. You can borrow one of mine," I said immediately, apparently opening my bag to bring it out. "No, no, don't bother yourself," he snapped. "John is sitting at the back. I'm going for it," he said politely and began to walk away from me before I could utter a word.

I knew what he meant, and I supposed he did the right thing.

She coughed a bit and added to it a humble smile. She looked straight at me. "I thought I have seen you already that day at the Chemistry lab," she said. There was a great deal of apprehension in her voice.

"You weren't bad in those formulas you applied."

"You mean me?" I questioned wondering.

"Yes." She nodded with smile.

"Aren't you Paul Basky?" A grip of suspense and surprise roped into my thoughts.

"How long have you been following me around without my being aware?" She didn't like that comment; I felt it the moment I voiced it. Sometimes, I just say a word that doesn't sound pleasant to people. It isn't that I have an attitude problem, but somehow, I love expressing my feelings the way I felt it. Most often I realize that the people I spoke against are hurt in a certain way.

"Did you say following you around?" she asked, looking humiliated. I quickly changed my mood and began to smile accommodatingly. "No, I didn't mean that. I was only surprised seeing you call my name when we have never met before. I am very sorry about that anyway."

She said, "We were all together in the lab yesterday where I spotted you for the first time. Or do you think . . ."

I interrupted her, "Please, you don't have to explain anything." "I am very pleased to meet you. In fact, knowing you at this point is my great pleasure," I said honestly. She seemed to be satisfied with that. She smiled.

"I suppose I don't need to introduce myself any longer. Maybe you can tell me your name," I requested. As my voice became more confident, I became the focus of her whole concentration.

"I am Laura. Laura Luthom."

The name rang a bell. I've always heard my dad discuss that name with his colleagues.

Mr. Luthom was my father's law colleague, and papa always said that he was a brilliant lawyer. He would talk about his performances before any Supreme Court jury. I also know that the Luthom he often speaks about was from a royal family, and he died many years ago. So, I wanted to know more about her. She was going to proceed when my curiosity interrupted her, "Are you from the royal Luthom?"

She unzipped her side pocket and brought out an ID card and gave it to me.

"This is my ID." She watched quietly as I gazed interestedly at the card. She seemed to possess a huge amount of confidence in herself. I raised my head, and our eyes met by accident. She leaned back and away from my face.

"What have you found out?" she asked.

"You are royalty," I said.

She nodded her head with a smile.

"You know what," I went on, "I was thinking of what it takes to be in the shoes of our parents. What they went through to become successful in what they do?"

"My dream is to become a qualified engineer. My dad is a lawyer." An ecstatic note of frighten suddenly drag on her face. I couldn't explain what causes that, but obviously, she was a bit upset. "People in this world are not appreciative, no matter what you do to help them. They would not appreciate your effort."

"I guess you owe me an explanation on that."

"No, don't bother to ask, please," she said emotionally. "Maybe we shall talk about it next time. Let's talk of something else, please."

I took another quick look at the ID once again and gave it back to her. "Thanks a lot."

She nodded with a smile. "My pleasure," she answered.

I planned to keep silent, not to invite any more conversation, and enjoy the rest of the bus ride home. My intention did not last more than few minutes before she broke the silence again.

"You know what," she voiced, "maybe I should say at this point that we have some things in common though we are meeting for the first time."

"Permit me to ask what you mean by that?"

"Can't you see it yourself? It is like we have something in common, but don't ask me what, because I will not be able to explain it to you. Time will make you see it." "Okay, if you say so," I replied.

"But you are a princess, and I am not a prince," I said jokingly, just to make her laugh about my attitude.

"Don't worry. I made you my prince already," she said and went on. "Yes, I may be a princess, but not everyone knows me as one. Besides, calling me that name reminds me of an old horror."

"I don't mean to hurt you," I replied. "But why is it that everything we talk about tends to hurt your feelings. I don't understand it? What's wrong with you?" I asked.

"I don't expect you to understand. After all we just met each other. We have plenty of time to know one another better. So don't worry about me."

She tong her lips and began to look behind me, a distinct motion that showed how much she cared to certify who that person coming behind me was.

Moji wrapped her hands around my neck from behind. I noticed it made Laura extremely jealous. Moji snuggled her face in the hollow of my neck and said with her usual tiny voice.

"Who is she?" she queried in my ear.

"Someone special to me!" I answered in a low tone. She raised her head up to look at her. She nodded pleasantly with smile. Her voice broke out loud, "If anyone wishes to taste a chicken, let him go for a promising one." She nodded her head once again.

"Who I am looking at here isn't bad at all, this guy." She pointed at me. "He is not a novice about a good stuff." Laura broke into laughter. I shook my head in a funny gesture.

"Come on, we are just friends. All the same, meet Laura." She moved forward apparently holding onto the pole of the bus. "Absolutely divine to meet you," Laura said.

They shook hands. "Please call me Moji. I am his troublesome younger sister."

We laughed. She walked ahead to sit beside Laura.

"What grade are you?" Laura questioned.

"Would you like to guess?"

"Huh, well, I think you must be in grade four," Laura said. "And you want me to be surprised at that?" Moji said and shook her head in disagreement.

"Paul told you already."

"That's not true. We hadn't even spoken a word about you when you showed up," I spoke up on her behalf.

"Okay, I believe you," she said. "You are right, I am in fourth grade. What about you?"

"The same class as you—fourth grade (D)"

"I see," Moji said. "No wonder we have not met. I am not used to those guys in the Arts Block," Moji confirmed.

The bus suddenly stopped, and Laura stood up to get out of the bus. She stood in front of me and looked straight into my eyes with affection.

"I would have to step down here. It has been a nice ride all through with you." She turned to Moji. "Splendid to meet you, Miss Basky. I think you now have a reason to pass by the Arts Block sometimes. At least we find a friend in each other now." I stood up and gave her a peck. She quickly rushed down the stairs of the bus. We waved good-bye to her until she vanished from our sight into a side street.

Mike got down from the bus long before us. I didn't take note of him any longer in the bus. I know I owe him a whole sum of tease on Monday at school.

For the first time in my life, I had a feeling of affection toward someone outside of my family. It was something special what I felt inside of me. It had never happened to me before, and I wasn't sure of what to call it. I wasn't even sure of what I wanted from this type of friendship. She hadn't told me everything I needed to know about her, but somehow, I liked the challenges she posed to me and looked forward to seeing her again. Perhaps this was what other ladies lacked that had kept me far from them.

I always felt I did not understand ladies as friends. Therefore, my assessment of her turned to be a treasure of integrity.

For the first time in my teenage life, I was beginning to be unsure of myself.

CHAPTER TWO

*I*t was now ten days since I met Laura in the school bus, and since then, I have not been able to see her anywhere in school. Neither had Moji seen her. I thought they should have seen each other more often than me. The situation was like traveling along one's heart and slightly giving it a taste of unusual affection that needs to be renewed at all time but instead, it suddenly disappeared and left one to shiver around for just imagined love.

Of course, an important part of my character is my principle of keeping my worries to myself. It is a trait from my youth that has not changed. It means I pretend to be okay when I am truly not. In other words, I can hold my grief when something bothers my heart without anybody knowing about it. Some people may call it a stupid quality because it does not fit into their way of life, but the truth is that, everyone cannot be the same. We all do things in the best way and manner that appeals to us. In my case, it has been a merit that has won me a gold medal among many admirers.

A football tournament was about to take place that day, and everyone was looking forward to the game. I was going to witness the match live as it happened on our school football pitch. Being a Thursday, the lectures stopped early for the students to prepare for the match. One major reason why a large percentage of students are interested in the game is that in the previous years, schools have improved tremendously with their level of football, it has become more maturely and brilliant skills are on display for the spectators to enjoy.

The match is more competitive now, so we look forward to having a quality game from both sides. We have seen it happen so many times when the players from Pitterluck College would systematically dominate the entire match, forcing their opponents to chase a losing game. Nothing captures people's interest more than a good performance that produces goals, and such a performance easily takes the crowd by storm and into a sportive celebration. This match is not different. We were expecting to see new football potential in the players; no doubt the almighty Pitterlock boys often liked to prove to everyone that they are the better team, but this year, our team was ready to challenge them. And since they have been leading, they have never disappointed their numerous fans. So due to this great competition that was just about to commence between the two powerful football giants, the student spectators were dragged into commentary on who will carry the day. Students from various schools in and around Iyatan, venue for the great match of the day, were present to cheer the teams on. Even people from far neighboring towns came to enjoy the match so that they were not left out of the fun. It was tempting to conclude that Pitterlock will carry the day as usual, but a lot of students dared not make any prediction for this match because no one was sure of the outcome.

They have always put up a great performance, and from their past results, winning was traditional to them and their confidence was always high, so you can't spot any defect in the team. However, football is not mathematics; there is that mechanical accuracy that stood in the form of question marks in people's hearts. They weren't willing to outdate what they knew about the ever-ready St. Jones players of Iyatan. They knew what they could do on a good day, hence it was another poll of confusion that needed to be proved by the outcome of the game. Among other schools in the town, St. Jones, being a government school, has been the only school that has been involved in many competitions with major schools from other cities in the state and comes out victorious. They had traveled far northeast to play with other colleges. This helped them a lot to improve their footballing skills. Without stretching too far from reality, they had often won most of the competitions. Even the National Football Association (NFA) had acknowledged them among college teams for their unique performances in the past. For the first time since the history of St. Jones College, this happens to be a first leg completion they would ever have with any of the schools in the town. Therefore, it explains morally why St Jones playing against Pitterlock College drew so much interest and attention from the community.

All sides of the premises were jammed with different people of different ages, not just students from other schools alone, but all the football lovers of the town were there to witness this match. St. Jones school authority had declared that day as a half-working day for all the students. It was a liberty that gave every student of St. Jones the freedom to do whatever they wanted, as far as the remaining half day was concerned which was the afternoon session. According to the disciplinary law guiding the school policy, students living in the hostels were never allowed to put on casual clothing even for an event like this, and despite the fact that we were a co-ed school, it was not allowed for any student to have a boyfriend or girlfriend for any reason whatsoever on the college campus, at least it must not be known to the school authorities. In fact, it happened to be the most important rule, of the school disciplinary law guide, in the day-to-day running of the school. But as anyone would know this, no matter how effective a law may be, it would always have a leak somewhere along the line, either by the people who made the law or by the people whom the law is made for, in this case, the students. Therefore, in order to prove how special the football activity is, all students, regardless of what grade, gained freedom over the school rule for just one day; everyone was allowed to wear his or her home clothes to the match venue.

It was such fun, a great joy for all the students. The atmosphere was comparable of interstate sports competitions where people overcrowd the venue, and it was just great fun for every one present.

Boys and girls were seen around the school, with sounds of jokes in the air, having all the kinds of fun that greatly attracts recognition to the events leading to the game. Likewise, students from other schools in the town were not left behind in the bid to showcase their presence to make the occasion great.

It was an amazing atmosphere; there was room for those doing business selling snacks, drinks, and petty things for people gathered there. People with something to sell were making huge sales and profit, of course, from the crowd. Hence, if one had to make a comparison to their usual daily sales, it was no surprise that many of them wished that the sporting event was organized more often than once in a while.

For the traders, the game was not as important to them as the fast business they were doing, so making good money was what they were interested in.

Since I wasn't good enough in Mathematics, I was not able to determine the actual numbers of people that crowded the match venue. But from what I saw, the crowd could be in hundreds if not up to a thousand people in our school premises to watch a college football match.

The noise from the crowd was deafening, and it hastened my coming out of the boys hostel to join the crowd at the main football arena where the match was about to begin.

A voice called out my name from the crowd—Fredrick and Williams sat under the orange tree that provided a shade around the hostel park. It was a famous spot where most students relaxed during their free time from class, especially the boarding students who have it situated behind their hostel on the way to the sport's field. I walked to them with laughter on my face. "Moji and her friends left us few moments ago," Fredrick said as I approached them. "Where have you been? She is anxiously looking for you." I stood in front of them thinking of how to locate her, looking around the crowd trying to spot her. "Maybe she wants to hand over one of them to you," Williams interrupted jokingly. We laughed over it.

"How many were they?" I questioned, apparently directing my question to Fredrick. Williams fast forwarded, "Two of them and your sister. In fact, Moji told me secretly that . . ." "That what?" I questioned. Fredrick smiled. He tried to stop the joke, but Williams was ready again with his running mouth. "Nothing special anyway. She told me she'd have them ready for you to make your choice." He shook his head and went on. "Some people are too lucky to have a sister in the same school. It's a good way to rub the ocean. I wish I had one too," he concluded. "You know what, Williams?" I said at once. "What?" he snapped. "You mean one for me?" he said and laughed. "I am used to your jokes. The best thing is not to mind you. Silence is good enough for you." "Oh, come on! Don't do that. Don't be selfish with your fishes." "On a serious note," Fredrick said, "she promised to check back." "Really, thanks," I replied. The noise from the crowd rent the air again. This time, it was not a joke. I quickly jumped to my feet and made haste toward the noise of the crowd. Fredrick and Williams were not the football type. They weren't bothered about whatever direction the result of the match went. All they were concerned about was the general fun that was going on, which already created a lot of impact on everyone's mind.

The Pitterlock boys had begun to do what they know how to do best on the pitch, play good football. They have begun to network on people's mind, as they were not willing in anyway to give up their title that meant so much to their reputation. They were pulling the crowd away from the St. Jones players. Something I was not really happy about.

Though the field wasn't big enough to truly give the players an opportunity to display the true professionalism of their skills, the players from both sides were playing better than expected by the crowd, especially the Pitterlock players. Their movements on the ball are dazzling, accurate passes and dribbling is so perfect that it storms the crowd across the moon.

It went on like this till the end of the first half. No goal on both sides, but a good game to watch and an even score line was a better reflection of the game so far.

Anything can happen at any time in such a tight match, especially in a competitive game where nothing can fully be predicted. It happened to be the case in the second half when St. Jones players began to realize that their dream could come true after all if they could score a goal. They started playing better than in the first half.

No one could believe what was beginning to happen with their pattern of play, for nobody could easily accept the notion that things like this could happen with a mere application of different style of play. None, including myself, was able to understand how good St. Jones players were. I was sure the coach really had a good talk with the players at halftime.

They showed class in the second half. They were not only putting their opponents under pressure, but also threatening to score. Of course, they became very adventurous, and their opponents returned fire for fire. In course of doing that, they exposed themselves at the back, and St. Jones took that advantage to score the only goal of the match. The game ended in favor of St. Jones with a final score line of 1-0; unbelievable, but yes, they did it!

Despite the disappointment for the fans of the other school, some people felt it was a balance and fair result; the other team played better in the first half, and St. Jones were better in the second half and got the winning goal. The crowd maintained a standard of discipline from fans. There was no fighting, and every one maintained the peace for which I was very proud of my college.

CHAPTER THREE

The game was over, but the day was still young. It was rather becoming the enemy of the people, for nobody wanted the match to come to an end, but none can do anything about it, and nature must take its course.

It was already 6:30 p.m., yet it was as if the day was just starting. The atmosphere that now occupied the air was filled with intense emotions running high. Everyone was into all kinds of fun of their own. Fans of the winning team were jubilating on account of their victory, those on the side of the losing team were consoling themselves, and others were still busy analyzing the match in any way that suited them most. Nevertheless, the evening ended with laughter and in a friendly atmosphere without any negative incident.

I was beginning to get worried about finding Moji so that we could board the next bus to take us home. The first thing that came to my mind was to walk to my classroom and wait for her. It was the best decision I could figure out. I started walking toward the

Form Five blocks, where my class was, a short distance from the staff quarters.

A dream of a boy hoping for a brighter future suddenly flowed into my mind. It was an imaginary folktale of achievements which papa often spoke into my secret passion. A thirst for climbing up the ladder of luxury, but as much as I dream seeing myself on that chair of authority, I've never once thought of what it takes to get there and sit upon the throne. Though, I understand one has to study hard and go through extensive educational training and all that hard work, thanks to Grandpa I also know that achieving success in life goes beyond a professional qualification alone. Papa's lectures are like a type of vehicle which conveys me to a bank of respect among my friends, while Grandpa's poetic and metaphoric input is the invisible fuel I need to assure myself that there is a blessed journey ahead of me.

A hand came around my face from behind. It slowed my movement to a standstill. I know it was not Mike; he was the person that normally plays a joke like this on me. He had not been around; he traveled for the weekend to Sapele. I laughed. "Okay, okay. You won, I lost. Take the point I take the salute. Tell me who you are." She stepped forward as I tried to see clearly. It was Iluna, Mike's girlfriend. "Top of the day, friend," she said happily, still smiling. "Did Fredrick told you we were looking for you?" "Yes, he told me, but he wasn't specific." We continued our walk as we spoke. "Who is the other girl with you guys today?" I asked. "Guess who?" she replied, still looking bright. "Do I know her?" "Of course, you do," she replied softly. "Okay, we are talking of Laura here, young lady," I said with confidence. "How do you know?" she questioned, looking surprised. "I just happen to guess right, no big deal," I replied.

"Why must I even be surprised? After all you must've been dreaming of her since your last meeting with her?"

"Meet who?"

"Don't tell me what I know, guy. Before Abraham exists, there were men," she declared.

"Moji told you something." She shook her head, meaning no.

"Whatever goes on in this school is to my knowledge," she said and laughed. "Yes, I know that. You have people around working for you." I said jokingly. She laughed again.

She is a good laugher. She holds her stomach to express how deep her laughter is. "You are too funny." She touched my left shoulder to stop us from walking. She became serious. "Baby, it is getting dark," I said, interrupting whatever she had on her mind. "The last bus leaves at 8:45."

"Yes, I know," she said and went on. "I don't know how to tell you this, but let me start by telling you that she really loves you. She has not been herself all this while. I mean since you both spoke inside the bus last time. You know, women speak with each other a lot. So, don't be surprised."

"How come you know her better than I do? You seem to be sharing secrets with each other."

"Yes, she is my best friend since childhood."

"Well, thanks for this piece of information. I will do my best. But does Mike know her too?"

"Of course, what do you think? He has known her for a long time," she said.

I nodded my head while smiling. Now, I began to see what the story was all about, an arrangement to suit a purpose. This was what it is. Well, in any case, it's all fine with me. They played the shot, and it went through the net. I wonder how Iluna would've felt if I had informed her of my own feelings toward her friend, but I decided to keep my pride to myself and allow things to work out naturally between Laura and me. I place my hand around her neck, and we walked silently to the class.

"I thought the class was empty," I said to her. There was someone inside the classroom preventing the door from opening. "Who is that?" I shouted. Iluna stood behind frightened. I pushed the door once again, and it went open easily this time as though I need not have used my strength in the first place. No one is inside. "Maybe the door was stuck," Iluna said, standing beside the board and using a chalk to write on it playfully.

We didn't check the storage room in the class to see if the fellow who held the door shut was hiding in there. Otherwise, we would've find out before now that it was Laura and Moji who had been crafty in their own way. "Look at them," Moji said as she led the way out. The two were smiling as they came out of their hiding place. "You guys are lazy. We are stronger than you, and we scared you." "In which record is it written, and by who?" Iluna asked jokingly. "By the way, you guys vanished from my sight."

"We were also looking for you too," Laura said. "At a point, I almost missed Moji as well. The whole place has been too crowded," Iluna said as she walk towards the entrace window. Laura and Moji advance toward me, and we exchanged greetings. She looked into my eyes, and she felt shy. I pulled her closer to me, holding her by the waist, and she turned and fell into my hands.

"Moji," Iluna called, "let's make it to the bus station before we miss our ride and leave them alone. We have just few minutes to catch up with the bus." She took Moji by hand, and both of them dashed out of the classroom heading for the bus station.

"I've been looking for you since we last met in the School bus the other day," I lied. "Haven't you been coming to school?" "I never miss school even once," she replied. "If you were really looking for me, you would have come to check on me in my class, did you?" "No, I didn't." "Well, so how are you?" she asked looking into my eyes again. A great deal of feelings in them. "Pretty okay, except that I now spend much time with my books these days. My final examination is fast approaching. You guys in Form Four are not yet there to know what's going on." She was becoming free in her speech with me, I discovered. She moved closer and sat on my desk.

"I understand WAEC is coming up in two months from now." I nodded. "I know you are going to make it. Something tells me that," she voiced slowly. I laughed.

"Should I call you a fortune-teller or an astrologist?"

"None of it, when I see a serious person, I know one."

"Well, who am I to refuse that? It's a prayer in disguise," I said hopefully. I looked at my wristwatch. "I am afraid if we don't make it snappy, we may end up going home by other means," I said. Quite surpeisingly, we arrived at the bus station within two minutes left for the bus to depart. In any case, our trip home was one full of fun, glamour of joy, if I may say so.

CHAPTER FOUR

That day was a weekend, a beautiful Sunday morning. Moji and I were going to visit Grandpa as usual. We were so happy about it. The only way to make us angry was to ask us not to visit him on any particular weekend. We preferred whatever the substitute was, should rather wait till next time because Grandpa was great fun to be with, and he was very good in his world of poetry.

Grandpa lived alone in one-bedroom apartment, not like those kinds in big houses in Abuja, Lagos, or Ibadan. It was just a simple home to live in, and nothing was special about it, since Grandpa was not a fashionable person.

I will briefly open your mind to the outlook of my town, Iyatan. Though a town is a town in an African contest, yet there are many things to speak about Iyatan. It is a culture—and tradition-oriented town among other neighboring towns. It is not a big city where all kinds of amenities are present, neither is it a place where one would have any difficulties in counting the population. But it is a place that people, including tourists, visit and speak well of. The roads that lead to the town from the major cities are two, one from the south and the other from the north. It happens to be the one and only town among others which enjoys an easy link of roads to the express via Lagos.

Even though we are not on the geographical map of the country, it is a honor to let you know that we also enjoy the usage of electricity, piped water, hospitals, and hotels. However, it should not be compared to the bigger cities.

The people of Iyatan are not lagging behind in cultural development. Perhaps it is a law from the past—I still cannot understand why every house in the town has a drawing of the previous kings of the land, an ancient custom that explained the history of the land. I have once been among many youths who do not believe in the existence of spirits, ancestors, or any of those elements of spiritualism—maybe I could put it as "voodoo." At this point in my life, I would rather be the last person to believe in them. Yes, indeed, the only name that deserved to be worshipped and praised is none other than the true living God, creator of heaven and earth, the living God of the eternal glory, and king of all creations.

In my town, there is a river where no one is allowed to have a bath in except for newborn babies. It is an age-old tradition, before even Grandpa was born. According to him, a woman transformed to become the river, a fact of which I still don't have. According to him, elders in the land are not allowed to relate the tales to the younger generation like us. It is forbidden to do so. Whenever a child is born in the town, the baby will be bathed in the river. It ensures the child becomes a true son or daughter of the soil.

Likewise, when someone is sick, the water would be given to the patient to drink and bathe with for a speedy recovery. So far, it has been working for them.

Iyatan is surrounded by mountains on all sides of the land. Putting beauty into consideration, it brings out uniqueness in the way it forms an empire of its own, a beauty that commanded respect among other towns in the land.

Grandpa's home was closer to the king's palace. All traditional rulers in Nigeria have their palace situated beside a commercial centre, a position of business attraction in the town.

If not for the heavy downpour that stopped us from leaving home on time, we would've arrived at Grandpa's home before 9:00 a.m. that Sunday morning. Grandpa knows how to make us happy. He possessed much wisdom for bringing a child to maturity—a positive way of teaching us what life is all about.

It was 9:28 a.m. As per Moji's idea, we passed through the back door to surprise him. Grandpa liked jokes, especially such that surprises him. Amazingly, he also had his own plan ready in place for us. He stood behind the back door to frighten us as we made our way in. I guess he sighted us at a distance of his house. Moji, who led the way, fell on the floor and fainted. "Mama, mama," she shouted helplessly as she fell down. At first, Grandpa became confused. "Moji is dying," I shouted aloud in concern. "No," he answered commandingly, looking disturbed. "Get me some water with that cup." He pointed to a plastic cup on the floor. He began to pour it on her face. He shouted at me, "I pray you stop crying, boy. She is coming around. Why are you crying?" He looked at me angrily. "Hold her other hand. We must take her to the room. It is too hot here." He sat beside the pillow and placed her head on his lap. I took a position at the foot of the bed. He rubbed her head with a local ointment and began to say, "A child of love must not die in the presence of her father 'Ewo.'" Ewo means it is forbidden. "Otherwise, let such death take me as a replacement."

"Have you guys eaten?" he asked. "Because I made a hot pounded yam and egusi soup ready for you." "That's my favorite, Grandpa. Where is it?" I said with excitement. Moji raised her head to look at me. She smiled. "How are you feeling now?" I asked. She nodded her head, meaning fine. "Grandpa has something ready for us."

"What is it?"

"Something we like eating," I replied.

"I prefer tea and bread," she requested. "Everything is available. Everything is available, my children," he said in his usual old, tired voice, apparently standing up slowly to get them ready.

The time was 12:15 p.m.; I sat on one of the mats arranged in Grandpa's parlor staring at those weaving materials that often kept him busy. They are traditional Yoruba clothing that are used for all kinds of ceremonial gigs. The king of Iyatan and his chiefs do wear them always, being traditional clothing for elders. They are quite expensive materials. 'It could be a good way of making money if only I can also weave them perfectly like Grandpa,' I said to myself while staring at them. The strange thing about it was that he never allowed me to go near it. I don't know why. Such a lucrative business of this kind should be inherited by his children and even passed on. Grandpa walk into the parlor and saw me stairing at the weaving materials. "my child," Grandpa said, "be brilliant in the way of the white men. Read your books of their people very well. Be the first on the roll call. Get whatever grade that is needed to be obtained. Even don't stop at that, go as far as the highest level to achieve greatness in the way of the master's degree. One day, maybe when I am no more, you will be glad not to learn what I am doing now, a time when you will become one above the glory of the moon." He withdrew into his kitchen and came out with covered bows.

"This is for you, son," he said. I stood to collect them. "Taste it. You will judge the difference between this and your mother's food," he joked. "I know you cook so well, Grandpa, but I think Mama does it better, because it is her world." I said in the same joking manner. "If you take sides with your mother, I will accept that. After all, she gave you life."

"No, no, Grandpa . . ."

"Never mind, son," he interrupted, "you are my darling. I am proud of you both. Concentrate on your food now. I will go and get your sister food too. She prefers tea and bread." He stepped across the door to his bedroom. The food tasted so good that I could not stop until I emptied my plate in no time.

The entrance door that led to the parlor began to unlock itself. I couldn't see who was coming in, but I knew a stranger was stepping inside. I stood up at once to open the door cotton as to see who was coming in, but before I could stretch my hand out to do so, an old-looking man was standing in front of me with a face that reminded me of a man I saw in my dream a few days back. In fact, he had the same face I saw on that blessed night. He was an old man, about the same age of Grandpa. "Hello, sir, you want to speak to Grandpa?" I questioned. He nodded his head. "I want to speak to that great and only poet of wisdom. The only one Iyatan has ever produced." "Who the hell is he talking about?" I whispered to myself inwardly. "Okay, sir, I better call Grandpa for you." I took a closer look at the clothing he was wearing; it was "ofi," a traditional Yoruba outfit. The type Grandpa does. According to Grandpa, any chief that is dressed in ofi is an important eminent person in the society. Such person is always needed by the king. It is not all chiefs that are allowed to put on ofi, only a first-grade chief has the advantage of proclaiming the right to ofi materials in the society.

"Okay, my child, go and inform the noble father of yours." He began to walk freely into the house. "Go and inform Iduro-oye that the Olu of Iyatan is waiting for him."

Grandpa was very glad to have Chief Olu in his house. Both elders ran to each other and embraced one another. "The Oluawo himself," Grandpa started, "who sees him, don't know him, and who knows him, never meet him, a man who sees far beyond the eyes of a lion. Oh yes, without him, Iyatan has no history, and with him around is the fountain of joy to celebrate. Oluawo, it is you I greet."

I became more curious to know who this man really was. I stood quietly beside the bedroom door, making my presence not seen. I watched them exchange praises of one another. Their continuous laughter and embracement was enough noise to bring the whole town down. Grandpa proceeded joyfully to sit by his permanent weaving section where he normally sat when working on his materials or hosting a visitor. The Olu sat at a distance from him. "Iduro-oye," the Olu went on, "a man that dives into the unseen ocean of thoughts, and peacefully form a creation of mind from the spirit of imagination. People like you are not yet born, and the ones in existence are not yet living. They are yet to be found. You are the one." He pointed to grandpa in admiration. "You are the one that uses the waves of the sea to drum a chorus of poetic meaning."

He stood up smartly from the mat and brought out a piece of white chock from his pocket. "Here is the chock of life and prosperity." He raised it up into the air, and Grandpa touched it with his left hand on Olu's palm. "It is the saying of the elders that whoever that touches the chock of life brings happiness and prosperity into his home. And who taste the cola-nuts of 'Ogun' will not see the red eyes of 'laka aye' god of iron." He dipped his hand into his bag on the mat and brought out a four-side cola nut. He spit it into four equal parts and went on with his talk. "We all know the importance of cola nuts and the role it plays in our custom and tradition. It was the four sides of the cola nuts that resolved the problem between the great Okpela town and Iyatan in the past century. Hence, it was named the weapon of peace." "True talk," Grandpa said while nodding his head to Olu's wise sayings.

"As I speak now," the Olu said, "it is obvious that we are four people in this house, and it is very certain that we shall all have a gracious life." "Amen. Amen. Amen," grandpa agreed, rubbing his two hands together. "How does he know that we are four in the house?" I questioned myself amazed. He pulse a little. He split the chock into powder form on his palm and then blew it into the air.

In the same silent manner, He split the cola nut into four equal part, and gave some to grandpa. "Iduro-Oye, this one is for you. Eat them in peace. Enrich your whole family with it, including the barrister . . . . We are all proud of him. He is our child. Where are the others? These are for them." He gave it to Grandpa. "The Orunmila, the god of peace, forbid the stream to pass behind them. It is a must for them to overcome the power of their enemies."

"Ase . . . Ase . . . Ase," grandpa answered in typical Yoruba language, meaning, Amen . . . Amen . . . Amen.

"Paul, Paul," Grandpa called out, "come and have this cola nut and eat it for your health. We have all reasons to glorify God for bringing Chief here today." I did as he ordered. The Olu suddenly began to look at me with a keen interest. Gradually, a smile spread over his face. I never liked that. All of his talk all this while had already made me feel uncomfortable with him. Now, his looking at me had just begun to add to my discomfort. "Paul," Grandpa said, "bring me the keg of palm wine I kept beside the table in the room. You will find it on the floor." I put it down beside him, and I was about to walk back into the room. "Iduro-oye, allow this young man to sit with us," Olu requested. His voice slowed me down. I turned to look at him. "What a wrong request!" I said to myself. I had no choice, I was only a boy, and I must obey the voice of the elders. I took a place beside Grandpa, trying to make myself relax. A pall of silence dropped on everyone, but the Olu changed the mood again in no time. "Iduro, who is this young man?"

"My grandson."

"Your grandson!" he repeated wondering.

"This gentleman," he pointed at me, "I mean this good-looking man will be a king in a short time to come. Where have you got this noble and intelligent creature from?" Grandpa maintained his silence and watch him display on.

It is dramatic in essence, very superstitious but interesting to observe. He put his hand into his "Agbada" clothing and brought out a black traditional bids surrounded by cowries and began to display it on the floor.

I shot a quick glance at Grandpa; he seemed to be enjoying the whole thing. His concentration was more than I could tell. I guess that was why he was a good poet, with an ability to dive so deep into the creativity of mind. "Iduro-oye," he voiced and shook his head in disbelief. "You have something great around you, but you don't know it."

"May I ask what it is?" Grandpa questioned. The Olu smiled. "This young man," he pointed at me again, "is the globe of your family, a light of destiny that must have to shine whether they like it or not. He would shine around the world, a storyteller of a time to come, great poet of his own time, greater than you are spoken about today. He will be known by the white people across the Atlantic. They will appreciate his work so much that he will be referred to as the master of storytelling." He paused, looked at the bid, and shook his head. "What kind of person are you, my son?" He questioned with a surprising look on his face. I guess he wasn't expecting a reply from me. I am glad he went on. "No, they must be joking, my son," he said slowly while looking at the bids. "When the time comes, they will bow to the wish of God the supreme, father of all design." "Who are those people?" Grandpa asked interrupting "He would go through so much in life. Iduro-oye, remember, there is more to the night than the day. The people of the night would mark him for a target. They will do everything possible to stop him from the crown, but not to worry, the 'Eledumare,' God of the world, has a mission to fulfill in him. When the appointed time comes, Iduro, I repeat when the appointed time comes, all heads will bow to the commandment of the Lord. But before then, it will look as if the world is about to end on him.

"The good thing about him is that, he is a different creature because the crown will fit him only. No other can wear it. It is only for him! Another interesting thing about his life is that, his major enemies will come from his friends and his father's family. They shall be the people who want him dead, but the truth is that, his soul is not designed to be overcome by them. They can only disturb his finances till the time appointed." Grandpa took a shot glance at me, and I understood what he meant. I stood up at once and began to serve the palm wine into the two native calabash cups attached to the keg. I passed it over, and they set the ball rolling. "Pour some for yourself too," Grandpa said. "No, Grandpa", I replied. "What belong to the elders is not to be toyed with by a child."

"He is right," the Olu said, "let him stay off it. This is a drink of 'Obatala' the god of success. The boy's spirit does not drink it. He is the success of himself." I thought I could use the opportunity to get away. Anyone who was observant would have noticed how tired I was, but the Olu would not allow me to leave. I began to wonder if I was the purpose of his visit to Grandpa's home. I made another move. "Why are you leaving my child," he voiced as I stood up. "Please, my son, don't read a different meaning to my interest in explaining your future to you. 'Orunmila' sent me to you. I am not allowed to collect a pay for doing this. Sit down, my young boy, and be yourself." He went on, "I am going to make this brief as possible. Please, my child, this is the message for you. Never trust a friend. Not a single one. They are betrayals all around you. I can see it so clearly.

"The moment you entrust a little of yourself to the so-called friends, you are jeopardizing. The oracle goes beyond human imagination, my child. Never, I repeat, never doubt a single word

I tell you here today, because it shall come to pass." He turned to Grandpa. "Iduro-oye, here is my last word before I take my leave. Your grandson is preparing to travel to the land where his destiny begins. I mean the land of the white people."

"You mean him?" Grandpa touched me.

"Yes, your grandson, or is he not your grandson?" "As a matter of fact, he is. But how can that be?" Grandpa asked warily. "He is the only male child we have in this family. His parents are not prepared to send him that far from them, nor would I even buy such an idea at all."

"Oh yes," the Olu replied. "That is why the oracle never lies. 'Orunmila' said his parent would not like it for him. Then I was confused, but along the midst of my confusion, the oracle spoke again to me in proverbs that since the beginning of creation, human passion has climbed beyond the boundary of biblical laws, below the degree of eternal call, and to the level of human destruction. His parents reject the majesty he is destined for due to the fear of losing him to the storm of the world. But they also forget that when our Lord, king of the world, and heaven decrees a matter, he has to only say it, 'Be' and it shall come to pass. That is the case of your grandson. Definitely, without doubt, in a little time from now, the young messenger would begin to face his own reality, a journey that would make him a man of his own time," he completed and stood up from the mat.

I glanced at the clock on the wall. It was 6:15 p.m. Grandpa also stood up and began to walk by the Oluawo's side toward the entrance door. He bid good-bye to us and closed the door behind him politely. "That is the Oluawo of Iyatan," Grandpa said. "The only wise priest of our land. People from far cities come all the way to consult him. We should consider us lucky to have him visit us today. Indeed, it is the gods that sent him to you," he said, and he walked back to sit down. "Yes, Grandpa, I believe what you say. If not, why would he choose today to visit you? It means he knew Moji and I will be around you today." I shook my head in overall surprise. "He must be very powerful," I concluded. "Yes, he is, but a good man."

"But, Grandpa, why is he calling you a different name?" Grandpa looked at me and smiled. He put his arm around my shoulders. "Well, my name is Basky as you also bear, but Iduro oye is my chieftain title given to me by the late king of Iyatan. I was known for my good work in poetry."

"Wow, sounds good! You are a chief. I never knew that."

"Yes, my son, I am one of them by merit. Now listen, Paul, I think the time has come to pass this important message to you. A time is coming when you will need it to get going in life." He coughed and requested for some palm wine. I poured some for him, and he drank it all. He gazed at me quietly and went on, "This is advice, son. I hope it will find a place in your heart so as to be useful in time to come." He removed dirt from his eyes. Everything about him was slow; he was an old man. It astonished me to see how elderly people talk in such a creative manner. Grandpa and the Olu have a similar method of approaching the bench. Although the Olu never referred to himself in any way as poet, from the way he defined the image, I could not think of him as anything but a stylish poet. As Grandpa regained his strength, he went on, "I will be very specific, my child. Life has deeper roots to our existence. The spirit which reigns in the heart of man is so wield and that one cannot imagine how the creator manages it up. We cannot understand it because our mind is too low to conceive such details. We are nothing but creations that live and flit away in a matter of time. I will point out one among those spirits and which is the most important of them all.

"I am talking of that little nature of man, smaller than an ant in the eyes of men, but a great sin in the sight of God. It is nothing but pride. Anybody under the canopy of pride will fit perfectly into the gate of hell. My child, accept this lecture as the one and only precious commodity your grandpa has to offer you. Money is something, diamonds are something, but this one is going to win you the biggest treasures of all time, both in this world and the next. There are different kinds of pride. None of them do man any good. At any stage of your life, even when you have riches and fame, never see yourself as the most righteous person or to be called an island. Never put God away from you. It is the fastest path to destruction. I have seen many out there," he pointed across the door, "who wing their way beyond the shadows of human understanding. What is their end? Calamities and death. The best of creatures is one who calls himself nothing in the midst of plenty. They who see themselves worthy of sleeping below the feet of their own slaves, such people are those who inherit the next world. Do you know why pride is so great an offense to God?" "No, Grandpa," I answered. Prior to the last word of my sentence, Moji came out to join us in the parlor. She had been sleeping. I stood up to welcome her. She smiled and sat beside me. "I slept so long," she said. "What has been going on in my absence? What are you guys talking about?" She stood up and sank in the hollow part of Grandpa's laps. "Well, my daughter, I was just telling your brother about the treasures of life."

"Treasure, why don't you give them to me too?"

"Of course, you should also have it, but you were sleeping when I started. Anyway, if you lend me your ear now and also borrow me your attention, I will put those treasures in the safest part of your mind."

"Okay, Grandpa, I am all yours."

"My daughter, if anyone asked me the question I just asked your brother before you came in, do you know what I will probably say?" "What is the question?" she asked. "Grandpa asked if I knew why being arrogant was the greatest offense before God," I said. "No, Grandpa," she shook her head, "why?" "Because, it is an offense that began with the creation of man. An offense that started when the universe came into being. The king of evil refused to obey the command of the most high, our Lord. God does everything on purpose. He requested all the Angels, including Satan to bow in respect to Adam, our forefather who was created out of clay. All of them did except Satan, who refused to be among the company of the righteous." "But why did God ask Satan to bow down when He already knew him to be the devil?" Moji asked. "No, Moji," Grandpa said, "at that time, Satan was not yet a rejected one. He was the leader of the Angels. His name was 'Iblis,' but when he proved arrogant and saw himself as better and more shaped than Adam, he lost his Godliness and holiness. It fell off him automatically, and his title was replaced with the name, 'Satan—deceiver of mankind.'" "Huh, that is too bad. How could he do that?" Moji said. "That is why he was sent out of the kingdom of heaven. Therefore, whoever follows his way would also behave arrogantly in everything he or she does. So, my children always see yourself as the smallest of atoms that needs to bow in respect to everyone in spite of color, race, and wealth (poor or rich). If you take my advice and practice it in your private life, your heart will be crowned with joy and satisfaction all the time. A pleasure you can never know where or how it comes about. Mind you, I don't mean you should become a fool to become prideless, far from it." "Then how can one do it?" Moji questioned. "Don't worry. We shall extend more on this when you visit me again." He gazed at the table clock beside his weaving materials. "You see, it's already 9:00 p.m. You guys have to go to school tomorrow." He stood up from the mat and stretched his tired body. "I will also tell you a story, 'Tears of a man,' a true-life story of a man and his pride." "Hmm, sounds interesting!" I said. "I can't wait to hear the story." "I know. I know," Grandpa said slowly as he walked into his bedroom. I felt so comfortable on the bed like I had never been. I was tired. I dozed off so fast, leaving Moji chattering. But the bad thing was that I forgot to say my evening prayers.

CHAPTER FIVE

The Onigba Park is a strange place to describe. It is situated at the far east of Iyatan, an isolated part of my town. I could not imagine why Laura had chosen this place for our meeting. But whatsoever, I read no particular meaning to it.

The long bench beside the gate was carved in an old-fashioned style. Since I was the first to arrive at the spot, I sat on it and looked around. The many shade-giving trees made it a peaceful atmosphere to relax in. It looked more and more like a place specifically designed to rest and relax in; it was quite comfortable. There was a narrow path that led the way into the park. One was easily transported into nature with the sounds of singing birds and other animals filling the air; it is a nice melody to be among nature. I glanced at my watch; it said 10:45 a.m. Laura had not yet arrived; she had not shown up as agreed. It had taken me some time to find the place, as it was my first time there. I had done all I could to leave home early and was still here all by myself.

"Are you waiting for someone, my son?" a voice suddenly sounded behind me. I jumped up from the bench tense.

"Yes," I replied with a frightened voice, nodding my head to confirm my answer at the same time. He was an old man, probably in his eighties. His face looked tired but calm. He shook his head and began to smile warmly at me.

"And you, sir? Are you also waiting for someone here?" I asked back, trying to sit back on the bench after the initial shock. He sat next to me on the same bench. "This park is my home. I have no other place. You said you are waiting for a friend. There she is."

He pointed to Laura. I was surprised. "How could he have known that I was waiting for a female friend?" I thought to myself. I stood up to welcome her.

"Sorry, I kept you waiting."

"Ten minutes is not so long," I replied. I turned my back to introduce her to the old man, but to my surprise, he was gone. It was very strange indeed. He just vanished into thin air. I began to think of it. It is not possible for an old man of his age to walk so fast away without noticing him, leave alone totally vanishing from my view. "It is unheard-of," I said silently to myself, but the good thing was that, I was with the person I was expecting, other things were less important to care too much about now. I had better call a spade a spade; the old man was just some distraction I said to myself.

I noticed she had a good knowledge of the geographical location of where we were. She probably had visited the place before; all the direction in the park was not new to her. She was looking very attractive in her clothes: tight blue stretch jeans that brought out her nice-looking curves and a long-sleeved blouse that set off her breasts. Her hair was neatly combed to the left side of her head. For the first time since I came in contact with her, I began to see her beauty which increased my feelings toward her even more.

The Onigba Park comprised beautiful flowers of all kinds, most of which I did not expect to find in a isolated place like this. Among the flowers was queen of the night, which was found all over the park, giving it a sweet fragrance. There were little ponds that stood at every joint of the park; in them were colored-fish, big and small. No one was allowed to catch the fish in them, and also, no one was allowed to hunt the animals in the park. It was conversation of nature at its best.

"So, what do you think of this place, Paul?" she asked as we walked toward the middle of the park. Her face brightened up with joy.

"Impressive, very impressive," I replied. "How did you discover this place? No one has ever mentioned this park to me," I said, while holding each other by the hand. She seemed comfortable holding my hands and was smiling. "My mother told me about this place. It has a special place in her life and makes her one of the happiest women alive." She let go my hands as we walked further to a nearby tree. She plucked one of the flowers and smelled it as she walked back to me. "Hun, so real of nature,", she declared, "Check it out" I perceived it.

"Let's sit over here," she pointed to the shade of a tree. We sat on the floor, well comfortable linking arm.

The wind continue to blow on us fresh air, and the branches of the trees began to fall on us in a peaceful melancholy, striking on the birds that were flying around as they try to hang on their various nets on the trees. No trace of any human being was seen around the place, except for the old man who disappeared. It was as if we were left alone to discover ourselves. Slowly, without a word, we held each other close and lay down on the grass floor. I began to kiss her, and she did not object to my advances as if there was no other day for it. It became so intense that we suddenly had a great desire for sex. She quickly began to unbutton her blouse and exposed her breast to my sight. I did the same to my scout T-shirt, exposing my bare chest to her. We held tightly to each other, and probably, we were in the same mood. Though, all of this was new to me, I played along, but I didn't have the confidence to continue. Somehow I felt I was confused in my head, so I stopped. Laura was in the mood, and she was not willing to let me go just yet.

She put her breast in my mouth, and she persuaded me to suck it. I did as she asked, and my mouth was all over her breast. The more I sucked her breast, the firmer they became and stayed pointed at me. It was an experience I would never forget. She dragged down her jeans trousers and pulled off her pant instantly and exposed all her private parts to me; honestly, I didn't know what to do except to follow her teaching in the school of lovemaking. Slowly, she brought me out of my frightened virginity and turned me into a courageous and confident young man. I have learned the skill of how to satisfy a pretty loving girl like her. She was on a higher frequency than me. She quickly helped me to unzip my trousers and began to rub my private parts gently. I had an erection making me to see the centre of an ocean. She inserted it in her mouth gently and began to suck on it. It felt good. I felt carried away and began to feel a stronger erection. "Please, baby, come into me. I need you now, please," she pleaded with me. With my very stiff penis, I mounted her, and she guided my length into her. I began to follow her instruction to move faster in and out of her. The shocking thing was that I was really doing so well than I thought possible during a first time experience. It was like a magic. My erection was getting stronger and longer with every minute passing by, and she could not help making a whole lot of pleasurable noise that made me to believe that I had become a man now. To prove myself well enough to her, I inserted it through her back, doggy style, and she was enjoying every bit of my aggressive action on her. I was practically experiencing what I learned in my biology theory class at school. At a point, she had reached her climax and could not stop coming again and again, but I just could not stop doing it since I had not ejaculated yet but at last, I did. I didn't use any form of protection. We didn't even consider the use of a condom; it all happened so fast. We did enjoy it. It was nicer the natural way, but we thought about it afterward and prayed that nothing serious happened to her. We just believed that since it was our first time, we were safe.

We lay beside each other half-naked, with arms crossed on each other's chests.

"I would like to carry your child someday," she said in a low tone. "I would like to live the rest of my life with you."

"Time will tell. Time will tell, my love," I replied.

We were both tired. The wind was still blowing from the southwest of the park into the town; it was a cool breeze. In this little time, we had developed something in common. I could feel her pain and sorrow. Again, she broke the silence. "Where my fate does lay with you?" she asked. "Lays together before we knew each other. Our good Lord knew we shall meet one day. He knew that by His grace we shall be wedded to one another when the time comes. But as for me, I will love you, respect you, and stay with you till death do us part." She raised her head and gave me a long-lasting kiss. "My body and soul shall be for you till eternity, my love," she concluded and laid her head on my chest. I suggested we begin to dress up as someone may walk past us to see us half-naked and we could continue our walk further in the park.

"Oh, I almost forgot," she said. "I brought some biscuits and two bottles of Fanta in my bag." She brought them out. We sat by the small flowing canal. I knew it was the right time to ask the questions I had always wanted to ask her. I've waited long for this moment; hence, I was ready to make use of the opportunity. I looked at her in the face. "Promise me something, Laura," I said, apologetically. "Anything for you, my love, anything," she said.

"Promise me not to cry when I ask you questions about your family. I feel we need to know each other better, especially now that we are intimate and our relationship is growing to be more than . . . Okay, tell me about your father. How come you are from a royal home?"

She laughed aloud. "I always knew you will ask me this question some day." She folded her right arm around my neck. She was straight and bold in her response. "I often say to myself all the time, 'May the Lord Judge the wicked people in their own coin.' Of course, my father was Barrister Jesyma Luthom as history recorded his greatness." I was shocked and surprised, but not in an obvious way she would notice. She went on, "I am his only child." She was again close to tears in her eyes, but she remembered her promise and quickly wiped them away. "I'm sorry, accept my sympathy," I said. She nodded. "What about your mother?"

"She's at home. Poor woman, once a happy mother, now, has no other choice than to obey whatever they say."

"Obey who?"

"You see, Paul, it happened some ten years ago, when our royal dynasty was threatened by the Mynslow dynasty. The Luthom was supposed to be the next king of Iyatan after the death of the last king, but instead of passing on the crown to the next dynasty, Mynslow family decided to grab the throne once again, thereby throwing away the royal oath. In line of succession, my father was next in line to the king. Everyone knows this. It is no secret in the town. But the question was, how can he ascend the throne when the ruling family still wants to retain the crown? They did all they could to retain it with money. My father and his brothers took the case to court, a legal battle that ended in our favor. My father was a wizard in law, a senior advocate of Nigeria. Everyone, including the eight judges, respected his brilliance when it comes to legal matters. The only thing he knows how to do best and the game he was born into was law.

"The Mynslow hired twenty-two lawyers to defend them, but despite that, my father and two other lawyers displayed brilliance and won the case outright. It was two different things." "So, why is . . ." "Why what, my dear?" she interrupted me. "This world is full of evil. They are always not willing to see the light shine. I wish the decision of the court was the final battle. Unfortunately, it wasn't. It took a different twist. This time, a fight between brothers broke out. An unpleasant confusion in the family." She shook her head as she stared at the river. I snapped and asked her to stop the story, but she refused. I hugged her close to my chest again. She was glad I did, but she could not stop the story halfway. I think she wanted to get it out of her. "You have the right to know everything, Paul, just as you said. You are part of my life now and probably my future, everything that makes me happy now. I need to say them all. No matter how painful it proves to be in my heart. Do you know what happened?" She raised her head to look at me. "They killed him. They killed my sweet father, a human right activist who has fought for others but nobody to fight for him. I still remember the last time he said goodnight to me. He used to call me his heart's princess. It was the last night my mother and I ever saw him alive. He slept and never woke up. That was the end between him and us." Tears began to roll down from her cheeks. She couldn't hold it any longer, and I could understand that. I wiped away the tears with my right hand.

Moji promised to pick us up with taxi by 3:00 p.m. It was about time. We started to move toward the gate, and there she was waiting for us with the cab.

CHAPTER SIX

What a pleasant surprise, Papa is in town visiting us on Thursday! We are happy to see him because it is unusual for him to come home on weekdays. I wondered what the reason was, but we were happy to have him at home. Both papa and mama sat in the parlor engaged in a discussion while Moji and I arrived from school.

"Wow," Moji shouted as we walked in, "Papa, you are early this week!"

"Of course," Papa said, "I am home to see my darling children. How was school today?"

"Quite interesting," I answered.

"When did you arrive?" Moji asked. I began to leave for my room to change my clothes.

"About two hours ago."

"And have you eaten already?"

"Moji," Mama snapped angrily. "Will you walk inside and get out of your school uniform immediately, and don't start asking those questions. You are not his wife."

Papa kept smiling. "Is it wrong of my daughter to ask after my welfare, especially my stomach?"

"What kind of question is that, not when she saw me at home?"

"She is a teenager you know. She's only concerned for her daddy. Remember, we need to bring her up in love and affection."

"I know," said Mama, "but I still have my authority in this house as their mother. By the way, what do you say about Papa?" she changed the subject. "Oh yes, he sent for me. He requested that I should be in town today."

"But why? What is the problem that cannot wait till the weekend, or is it something that serious that needs urgent attention?"

"Well, I don't know myself, but let us not worry, I will see him tomorrow. Anyway, is the food ready now?" She stood up hurriedly and led the way into the kitchen. Papa stood up at the same time and walked into his study room. "Paul," he called me.

"You called me, Papa?"

"Yes, my boy, please sit down." He pointed at the chair opposite to him. "How are your studies going? Is there any problem with them?" He questioned, looking at me directly in the eyes.

"Obviously not, Papa. All is quite well with me."

"Can I be sure of that?"

"Of course, Papa, I've never disappointed you before, have I?"

"In case you need me, any time, just let me know at once. Lagos is not a distance from my responsibilities, okay?"

"Yes, Papa."

"Sweet heart," Mama shouted from the kitchen, "you want to take a shower first before your food?" "Yes, good idea," he replied. I stood up and walked to his bookshelf. I picked one of the books, titled *The Law Report '86—Volume 10* and began to glance through it while standing. He looked quietly at me. "What do you like to become in life, Paul?" he asked.

"How do you mean, sir?"

"I mean what profession would you like to study at the university?"

"Civil engineering, all my subjects are science oriented." "That's wonderful, you know." He walked closer toward me. "You and I share some things in common, the act of confidence is one of those things. I guess you took that from me . . . and where is Moji now?" he asked.

"In the kitchen with Mama."

"Okay, that's right." He began to walk into his bedroom. "Papa," I said behind him. He turned and looked at me. "Guess what?" I said and smiled.

"Please help me out," he replied in a joking manner.

"Our final examination (WAEC) starts next week, and my first paper comes up on Tuesday." The expression on his face was a mixture of joy and fear.

"You mean your final exams are here already?"

"Yes, Papa."

"That's strange, and what are you doing about it now?"

"Best of my ability, sir. I have my timetable ready. I study hard enough, and I leave the rest to God."

"Is just by the door, Tuesday is few days from now. Promise me you will give your best for the examination. Remember, this is your opportunity to proceed to a university of your choice where you can achieve your life's dreams."

"I promise, Dad. I promise with all certainty. I will do my best."

"Does your mother knows of this?" he asked from his bedroom door. I walked to his door, "Yes, Papa. She encourages me all the time."

"Good." He nodded in satisfaction. "But, Papa, there is this last question I need to ask you." He was busy pulling off his clothes over his head. "Yes, tell me."

"What do you promise me if I pull out the flag at the end?" His face went joyous in a stylish Yoruba manner. "Without being told, son, you know what that would mean to your dad. Name it, anything you want, will be yours," he pronounced. "What a promise, Papa!" I said. "And wait to see how a man can be a master of his word." He tapped my shoulder and withdrew into the bathroom.

CHAPTER SEVEN

apa and Mama arrived at Grandpa's house at 11:00 a.m. on Friday morning. There were two middle-aged men, about the age of my dad; they sat beside each other on the mat in Grandpa's sitting room. There was suspense, and they looked angry, but they gave nothing away. Papa could see it immediately he set eyes on them. The Olu of Iyatan was already seated opposite to Grandpa, expressing a smile that invited a visitor into the house. Grandpa stood up to welcome his son and wife into his house in a Yoruba cultural way of love. Papa greeted everyone around twice, and he took his seat next to Grandpa. Mama had to do that in a different way. She had to add some additional value to her greetings by kneeling before them, a sign of respect by a Yoruba woman, and they said a short prayer of blessing for her. She then proceeded to sit beside her husband. The look on Mama's face was easy to explain. Apart from the fact that she was not comfortable in the midst of the old men, the thought of what the discussion was all about could not stop ringing in her head. She stood up at once, apparently in a mood to walk out of sight.

"You have done well, my daughter," the Olu said, "'Orunmila,' the god of divinity would bless you for the respect you have accorded to us, but we need you to stay around too. We need your opinion on this matter we want to discuss, especially since it has to do with your very own person."

"I think we should begin to break up the shell to see what lies in it," Papa said patiently.

"Yes, my son, I presume you must be surprised about my message to see you in the town on a short notice before your usual visit on Saturday. The word of elders says that, a discussion that is meant for the night cannot be held in the morning."

"But how long must we wait to wander to and fro with all these riddles," Papa said anxiously. "Don't you think it is better to uncover the claw at this point?"

"Very well, my son," the Olu snapped. "It is the saying of our elders that no matter how terrible a matter maybe, there is enough room on earth to accommodate it." He paused to clear his throat. "These two gentlemen in our midst are the representatives from the king. They are here to look into a matter that involves your son, Paul, and a young girl from the royal family."

"My own Paul?" Mama questioned wonderingly. Looking disturbed and uneasy, Grandpa maintained silence and watched the matter unfold.

"You must've heard of the mystery of the only park in Iyatan, a place of love and hate. It is the home of the Onigba gods. The mystic spirit of bond that brings two heads together in the name of love. No couple is allowed to visit the park except they understood the effect of violating the rules of the park." The Olu shook his head.

"Do you understand the meaning of my long explanation?"

"Not really, sir," Papa answered.

"It means people of opposite sex that visit the park must have to marry each other no matter what it is. If any of them violates the law of the Onigba gods," he shook his head, "he or she would undergo a terrible illness, an affliction that would last for a long time, before the violator dies."

Nothing can be done to reverse the cause. Now, the problem is your son and Laura, the daughter of the king, were found in the park under an oath of togetherness. A pall of silence fell upon everyone. Papa for once was not willing to buy into the story. He had enough confidence in me, but considering the caliber of people who were there to narrate the story, he began to feel uncomfortable with himself. One of the visitors from the palace pointed to Mama.

"What is it Tinuke?" Papa drew close to her. "Will you kill yourself over a story we have not yet confirmed from our son, and if that is even the case, what is the big deal about this?"

"I can't bear losing my son," she said softly.

"No one is losing anybody," Papa said in confidence. "There is a solution to it. We need to talk about it," one of the visitors said while still sitting. "Iduro-oye," the Olu spoke, "Please get me some water in a small calabash. I need to give her some herbs to drink." The Olu knelt beside Mama who was staring at the water mixed with some concoction. "Don't worry, my daughter. After drinking this, you will get well." She drank the warm salty water and began to doze off. Papa brought her into Grandpa's inner chamber. "She shouldn't be around when we discuss a matter like this," Papa said angrily as he walked out of Grandpa's inner chamber. "It is a mistake, my son," the Olu said as he tried to sit back on the mat. "Anyway, with the herbs she has drunk, she will get better soon."

"Well," Grandpa said, "I believe strongly that some time should be given to my family to think over the whole issue. After we have reached a decision, we shall send for you all again."

"That is thoughtful of you, sir," Papa said, "but I think prolonging this matter will not be necessary. It is simple and straight forward. The children mistakenly fell under the law of the gods. If there is no other solution than for them to be married to one another, so be it. We better start preparing their minds for the task ahead of them. That is what I think is the right thing to do now." "That is it," one of the visitors said, "that is exactly what the king wants to hear. We should thank God that the case is not the type of an abomination where it involves a brother and a sister. So, I don't think this is a matter we all need to be worried about. We have an understanding."

"And you think this is your final decision on this matter?" Grandpa asked Papa worriedly. "Don't you think we can reach a better and a noble solution if we give it time to deliberate on it?"

"I still don't see anything wrong with what I said, Father. Remember, we need to talk to Paul about the matter first, but if in any case he confesses to me, then I suggest we invite peace into their lives than to be thinking of a solution that could take time and be destructive in some ways. That boy is so precious to me. I will do anything to keep him out of danger."

"Very well, you all have spoken well," the Olu said, "and if that is the general decision here today, I also agree with it. There are some rituals that must be performed for them. So we just . . .'

"It has not come to that yet," Papa interrupted, "I need to speak to my son first. The problem is that I will not say a word of it to him now until after the next three weeks."

"Why?" the Olu asked. Everyone stared in surprise.

"Because he is about to start his final examination at college for which we have been preparing him for a long time. I have given him confidence and courage to do his best, and he gave me his promise last night on it. I certainly will not jeopardize his effort now. As a father, I want him to concentrate for this examination and do it once and for all. I have once been there, I know him too well. He is very emotional, and any form of distraction will break him down. Any little worry could cause a big difference for him."

"This is not acceptable to me," the guest seated on the left-hand side said, showing some anger on his face. "We all have children that go to school too. It doesn't mean we cannot talk to our children when urgency demands it."

The guest seated on the right-hand side nodded in support. "Maybe, because we see the value of education in a different way, we must not fail to understand one basic point here. We are all different people with a different approach toward life, and you don't expect me to do things in the way you want it. Do you?" Papa asked angrily.

"This is enough," the Olu said. "We must not allow the prince of darkness to overthrow our Godly sense of reasoning. I think Paul's father has been very considerate in this matter. I don't think it is right of us to deny him his fatherly right to help his child with his studies. The important issue has been settled. It is left for him to decide when and how to proceed with the agreement, and that would be on a later date." He got up, a sign that the meeting was over, and he turned to the visitors. "Together, we shall relate the outcome of this meeting to the king." He concluded and gave a long smile to Grandpa and Papa in the form of greetings.

"When she wakes up," he said to Papa, "let her have some food, and once again mix this in warm water for her to drink." He collected it.

"Thank you very much, chief," Papa said and smiled. "Your leadership will continued to be valued in the land." Olu accepted the gesture and quietly walked out of the house.

Although the two guests were not in support of the Olu's decision, they had to pretend to be okay with it. Olu is the spokesperson for the king in the town. Whatever he says or decides is what the king listens to and accepts as verdict. So, it is a challenge for them to accept the decision. They stood up, exchanged pleasantries, and walked off into the street.

Mama woke up after an hour of rest. All she wanted to know was the outcome of the meeting, but it took her no time to understand that her husband has used his legal professionalism to arrange things in a peaceful manner.

Chapter Eight

*I*t was 9:00 a.m. on Tuesday morning. All students had begun to walk their way into the school compound ready for their exams. What appeared to be a professional monster around was the presence of the so-called WAEC examination that stood horribly on the shoulders of all final-year students, including myself. The truth about it was that we were made to believe too many frightening stories about the WAEC exam, stories about the significance of passing it, and the outcome of what could be the fate of whoever fails it. They were just too heavy to let go, especially on those students who believed in hard work. They were not willing to compromise on their ability or fate toward their vision. From what I later understood about the examination, it was nothing special than other exams we have been doing. A failure or success of a man in any field of choice mainly depends on what he believed in, and his ability and confidence to go for it.

My heart was beating faster than normal, but I know it was not going to be the end of the world, though. As a matter of fact, the

strange look on everyone's face was quite enough to make anyone
sick, no matter how brilliant one might be. There had been no more
lectures for the past one week. All final-year students had been
left alone to wander around in their own fate, to engage in self-
preparation and wait for the D-day to arrive. "What's up, big boy?"
Mike shouted from a little distance behind me, as I walked across
the parks in the premises.

"Do you also feel the same heat?" He said and laughed.

"I am not going to hang myself for this, home brother. We shall
go inside and do the best we can," I said. "None of our teachers are
in the school," he said.

"What do you mean, who is going to invigilate the exams?" "I
overheard some retakes say teachers from different schools would
do the job here this time around, while our teachers have been
assigned to different schools."

"But if that is the trick, we are yet to see any of those new
teachers around," I replied.

"Perhaps they are in the staff room holding a meeting or just
chatting." He shook his head. "Whatever it is, the first paper
starts 11:15 a.m., and somebody must have to take control of the
examination hall," he assured. Guess what, twenty minutes to kick
off time, twenty-three policemen were stationed in the entrance to
the examination hall. "We are not expecting it to be that serious.
What difference is it to our usual class test?" I questioned myself.
Maybe there is more to it, because the ceremony is just too much
to frighten any student. No bags or any private belongings were
allowed in the exam hall. We had to walk in with only writing
materials and drawing equipment alone. Every student was properly
searched and confirmed fit to avoid any form of cheating. I guess,

no student will think of that; with policemen on ground vigilantly watching every one, it will be stupid to try to do anything funny there. I began to realize what Papa truly meant by those fears he was entertaining. According to him, this was the gate way to my accomplishment in life.

Two gentlemen walked in to the exam hall, and they introduced themselves as our examiners who were to watch over us as we commence the examination. They were teachers from Imo state. Honestly speaking, the look on their faces did not speak any friendliness at all. The only meaning to it was how much they meant business with us. They made it very clear to us that they were not going to allow any form of cheating or students passing answer sheets to one another.

Some students already thought of doing that, but with this warning, we knew it is going to be a tough battlefield. Also the presence of policemen watching around the examination hall defeated all plans the students had in their heads. Any attempt to cheat had been aborted, so we just needed to concentrate on the exams and do our best. The entire WAEC examination days lasted for three weeks of tight security both in and around the examination hall. No student got the chance to cheat on the other, except following the lay down rules as expected. People with thoughts of working over an expo were totally disappointed in the way things turned out. Well, according to Grandpa, life is how you choose it to be; hard work and concentration have its own merit at the end of the day.

CHAPTER NINE

*P*apa took a long, deep breath again and again while gazing at me mysteriously. Something was bothering him. I know something was wrong, but I can't lay my finger on it. He had been acting very strange for few days now. It had been two weeks since he started with this attitude of his. Is just that I couldn't allowed whatever is happening to be my worries for now as I continue my examination, I kept my composure all through the exams. I've always believed it had something to do with his office workload or stress from so many cases he had to handle each week. Maybe he was just tired, but now that my exams had gone out of sight, I felt it was now time to confront him and ask what was happening to him. I was sitting around our dining table, close to the television set, having my lunch. Papa was quietly sitting on the round chair behind the dining table, pretending to be watching the television. It was his favorite spot to double-check on two persons at the same time. "There is nothing to worry about, Papa," I said aloud emotionally, "if it is about the examination. I've told you from on set, with your promises around my wall, there are plenty of reasons to have confidence in me." There was a bit of relief in the way he looked. He smiled. He always liked when people talked confidently to him. "That's my boy," he said, "but you know, that's not what is bothering me." He stretched his hands toward me, asking me to sit closer by his side. "I always have no fear about your performances any time, my dear."

"Let me guess what." I fast forwarded the conversation since it was becoming interesting to him. "Okay, let's hear what you have for me." He placed his hand on my head lovingly and relaxed himself as he faced me head to head.

"I think you are likely facing some challenges with your cases these days."

"I wish you are right, but it isn't my cases. Besides, even if that is the problem, a man cannot run from his shadow. One must learn to be a warrior all time and face every battle."

"Then, what is the problem with you, Papa?"

"You are my problem, nothing else but you." A dose of smile mixed with fear twisted my bowel. For the first time since I grew up to know him as my father, he made me to feel a real challenge and worry in my heart. I looked at his face one more time and read a sign of mixed feelings on them.

"Is that why you have been around for the past three weeks now?" He nodded.

"I had to transfer my cases to my colleagues as to have time to be with my family."

"And the problem happens to be me?" He stood up. "Let's take a walk outside the house to the square," he said. Mama was not yet back from the shop, and Moji had also gone to school. So we had the whole time to our selves. Slowly, we walked along the tiny path via the town square. He placed his hand around my neck. "Paul," he broke the silence, "what's your view about life generally? What do you think about achievement and the way to do it?"

"I think the way to it is to study very hard, take my education more seriously, and to obtain a degree on one's chosen line of career."

"Yes, you are right, but there are those irrelevant things that can be an obstacle for achieving such height in life, do you know them?"

"Maybe like not being serious with one's studies, and to accommodate bad influences from people around, I don't know, but there are many things." We arrived at the square, and we sat on one of the wooden benches around the football field. "You see, my son, when I was at your age in school, being the only child of your grandfather, I was comfortable at home and at school. I was provided with all I needed to make things easy for me. I happened to be among the best students in my class. Of course, there were many distractions from all sides, such that could turn a serious student into becoming a block-headed one. I kept my head down. One of those things that could distract a male student is woman." He stopped and looked at me. I saw a note of seriousness in his words and written over his face; he was dead serious this time around. He meant his words, and he was bringing it across with the best logic possible. He was a brilliant lawyer; he knows how to develop his point.

"Is there any woman or a lady in your life that is affecting your mind at the moment? A woman who could distract you and pull you off the set out track, is there any?" He stared at me. I was totally silent and probably caught unawares.

"Am still waiting for your answer," he said slowly. "I know you have something to tell me. No matter what it is, you know you can count on me." He finalized and waited for me to respond. I nodded to signify yes. Almost the same time, tears began to gush out of my eyes. I became helpless than to speak out the truth. "Yes, Papa," I said, "there is a girl I like very much. She is a good girl, and she has not been a bad influence on me."

"What is her name?" "Laura, Laura Luthom." He put his hand on his chin and breathed down. Why this strange feeling, I don't know. But something told me I must not hide anything away from him. "No matter what his mood is, I need to tell him the whole truth. He is my father."

"How old is she? And what class is she?"

"Nineteen. She's in class four."

"Luthom is a big family, which of the Luthom are you talking about?"

"She is the daughter of late Dr. Jesyma Luthom." He was surprised at my mentioning that name. "Senior advocate Jesyma Luthom?"

"Yes, Papa."

"How long have you known her?"

"Barely six months," I lied. "And how will you describe your feelings toward her?"

"She is very positive. I like her because she does advice me a lot. Above all, sir, I love her, and she loves me too. We love each other."

"Did I hear you say love? What do you know about love? How can you recognize if someone loves you or not?" he questioned and continued to look at me.

I tried to be bold; I had to if only I need to get rid of the horror that could bring Laura and me apart. "Papa, I know what love is. I can write volume of pages on what I call love in my own way, at least enough to describe myself when I'm in one. It's a situation when my heart burns, burn for a girl whom I care for. I can go on and on to describe it, but you might not understand, Papa, because . . ." "Because you gave birth to me," he snapped angrily.

"Sorry, Papa."

"And how do you know if she has the same feelings for you?"

"Laura, she does, Papa. She loves me more than I do. She once told me that all that makes her happy was me, because since the death of her father, she and her mother knew no joy any longer."

"Where is her mother living?"

"In the palace."

"I see." He shook his head. "Does Moji also have some kind of boyfriend too?"

"No, Papa. Moji has nobody, but she is a friend of Laura." He smiled. I wasn't sure yet if that was to my favor or not. He went on.

"Someone lied against you." I raised my head to look at him. "They said you went to a park with her."

"A park, which of the park?"

"Which of those parks have you visited?" he asked back. "The only one I went to is the Onigba Park." He buried his head at the hollow of his palms. He looked disappointed.

"Well, we shall stop this conversation here now. Go to Laura and inform her to have dinner with us tomorrow at 6:00 p.m. I want to speak with both of you."

"Okay, Papa, I will do so." We stood up and headed back home. This time our walk was very silent.

I found it difficult to predict my dad in this matter of Laura
and me. At times, he would act to be in support, and at another
time, he appeared to be the one crucifying me. Somehow, I was
beginning to learn more about my dad, how he applied authority
in a strict manner to protect his family. Mama had not yet spoken
a word on this matter to me, but I suspected that she knows about
it too. Usually, I knew her to be a disciplinarian that does not take
nonsense and a caring mother when need calls for it. I told Moji my
encounter with Papa on this Laura's issue. "What do you think is
going to happen now?" Moji asked with a worried look. We sat on
the chair at the balcony of our house to chat.

"I really don't know, Moji. I don't even know who told him
about us."

"Have you spoken to Laura about what you discussed with
Papa?"

"There is nothing to lie about. I told him everything about
us already. So whatever wants to happen, let it happen. After all,
we killed nobody." I glanced at my watch. It was 5:30 p.m., and
Laura was just on time. She was walking down the road on the
path opposite to our home. She smiled from a distance, and Moji
walked out to meet her. They embraced each other. I also went
to join them. We exchanged some kisses, and she sat beside me. I
welcomed her to my home as Mama called Moji to join her in the
kitchen to help set up the table for dinner.

"I hope your dad is not upset with somebody today or angry
with us," Laura asked.

"No, no, it won't come to that, but not under any reason must
you mention our lovemaking to him." "But any attempt to take
you away from me, I will kill myself," she said. "I trust my dad. He

only does what makes me happy, and all he wants to know is if the relationship is serious and we love each other as I claim to him."

"Okay, we shall see," she replied. The dinner was served, but my dad had not joined us on the table. My mum gave her go ahead to start eating first as he would soon join us.

"Do you like the meal?" Mama asked from the other end of the table.

"This is very delicious, Ma. Thank you, Ma. It reminds me of such environment from the past, Ma."

Papa joined us on the table. He did not speak much, but he was just listening to others discussing and enjoying his meal.

"How do you mean, my dear?" Mama asked.

"When my father was alive, we used to have a complete family like this to have dinner, and it was fun. I miss it."

"My sympathy, sorry about that. Time heals all wounds," Mama comforted her.

"I learned your late father was Barrister Jesyma?" "Yes, sir."

"I once met him in a court room, a complete gentle man of the jury. May his soul rest in peace." She burst into tears. Mama stood up and consoled her and made her to sit next to her. "Cry not any longer. Let the past belong to the past. You now have a new family that will never let you down. We shall fill your world with love." She placed her head on my mother's chest. "Would you please excuse us, Moji?" Papa voiced. She stood up and went into the living room. "I need to talk to you and Paul concerning the park you visited. Do you have any previous knowledge about what the place is all about?"

She looked at my face. "No, sir, it is just a playground to us."

"Have you ever seen children playing there?"

"Not really, sir. I was there once with my mother. I liked the beauty of the place, so I decided to visit there with Paul."

"Suppose I inform you now that you have brought a cause on yourself and Paul with just your one time visit, what would you say?"

"May God forbid, sir? Paul is the one I love so dearly. I forbid anything that will destroy us." She uttered allowed. Papa and Mama exchanged a glance.

"Well, my dear, what your father just said is a true talk. Onigba Park is not just a playground as you call it. It is a spiritual garden that is meant for couples only. And . . ." Papa interrupted, "Both of you have sworn an oath of togetherness, never to leave one another for another person. If any of you violate that oath, the consequence is severe. In fact, it is death. What do you think of that?" None of us could speak. I was short of words.

"You see," Papa said, "both of you are not ready for what you are talking about called love. You are still kids, but you have transgressed beyond your limit by going into that park."

"No, Papa," I replied immediately. "I love her very much, and if you and Mama permit us, I wish to have her as my future wife."

"I love him more than words can express, sir. If only you and Mama can understand what we share together, it is not our emotions, and we think it is our destiny to be together. So please don't stop it. I wish and pray that Paul will be my life partner and husband," she said.

"If only I got a chance on this so-called thing you called love or relationship," Papa said angrily.

"I would've put a stop to this nonsense. But with the situation at hand, let's see how your childish behavior will not bring either of you into trouble, the mystery of life itself. You are inexperience in this journey of love, and I just hope that you get through it in one piece."

He stood up angrily and left for his bedroom, leaving Mama with us gazing at each other. "This is a matter of life and death for both of you. The situation is bad enough, and do not transgress beyond your boundaries now. The devil has a way of playing with people's mind in this kind of situation. None of you must allow stupid ideas to take over your mind. Never allow it, I repeat," she said. "Okay, Mama, you have my promise," she said. From the look of things, it seemed that was the end of the discussion for the night. Since Papa left us, there was nothing much to say again than to wish Laura a good-bye bid.

"Greet your mother for me. Tell her I will visit her one of these days." She stood up also and walked into papa's room.

Moji and I escorted Laura halfway home. For a short while, nobody talked about the matter again. It was like my parents put it to rest or I don't know what was on their mind.

Fate had a way of working things right. After the encounter with my parents, Laura and her mother had become a huge part of my family. Mama was the happiest of all. Over the past few months, she had learned to believe that certain things does happen to man in life so as to arrange things somewhere else. Quite unbelievable, Laura had easily gained a free passage into Mama's heart. They now operates an open-door relationship with one another. She helped Mama sometimes in her shop, and most of the times, she would give her some business tips.

Her mother used to be a business woman too, and those tips helped her business to flourish until her husband was killed.

My mom was very fond of her. Papa on his own part could not help thanking me for the joy I have brought unknowingly into the family. Apart from the way the whole thing started from the Onigba Park, the situation in our family has made it to be an event that is meant to be. Laura's mother brought special gifts of law books for my father from her late husband's library, many of those books are not available any more in book shops, so they were most valued by my dad. They were so good to my family. Papa called those books as the secret to Barrister Jesyma's best performances in the court room. Guess what, I now had my own room so that I have some privacy in the house. I no longer stayed in the main house with my parents. I was allowed to have my room in the back self-contained apartment in our compound. Wasn't that so wonderful? Well, I liked it so much. In the first place, it gave me a recognition as the firstborn of the house. Papa promised long before WAEC exams to allow me to reside at the back house apartment when I do well with my final exams. What a coincidence, accepting Laura into my family now gave us some privacy to be together and get to know each other better! We can express our love to each other without anyone disturbing us.

We had unregulated time together to build our relationship, and we became more intimate. I also had a double-sized bed so she could stay over whenever she wanted to stay, and my parents had no problem with that.

We did the same thing we did that very first time in the park. It actually became a usual practice, and she liked it. She even taught me some other things I didn't know until I became a master of it all. All I did was just to satisfy her so we could be together.

Laura and I started with the journey of our life together, in fulfillment of our destiny. My parents requested she move into our home, but this demand was turned down by her mother due to her loneliness and fear of being alone. Her mother refused to remarry after the death of her late husband, so she lived with her daughter. She had become a source of strength for her.

Hence, she desired to remain with her until when the traditional right was performed to properly marry her at a later date. But in the meantime, she continued to pay constant visit to my home, and in fact, she made our residence her second home. She was welcomed always as a member of the family.

CHAPTER TEN

It was 6:25 p.m. on a Sunday evening. Mama was sitting by the musical keyboard in the sitting room practicing her hands on the piano. She had no knowledge of how to play the instrument though, but she was using the instrument to keep herself busy and learn one or two notes. Moji was reading in the dining room area. I think she was busy with her physics test book. She was preparing for her promotional exam to class five that would come up in two weeks from now. Physics was one of my best subjects, so when she had a problem on it, she knew that she can count on my support.

"Oh, big brother Paul," Moji screamed. "My God, I just forgot to inform you!" Mama raised her head to look at Moji.

"The school committee placed an information letter on the noticeboard that the WAEC result has arrived and it would be on display at St. Jones on Monday on the school noticeboard. That means tomorrow." She covered her mouth with her two hands to express her disappointment to have forgotten such vital information. My head throbbed with pain, and my heart began to pump faster in fear of what would be the outcome of my big boy attitude around the house all these while. Time runs out so fast. It had been about five months since I dropped my pen on the last question sheet in chemistry practical; now the judgment hour has come.

"Is that so?" Mama said. "In that case, I will give you a ride to school tomorrow."

"No, no, Mama," I quickly answered, "that wouldn't be necessary. I will go on my own later in the morning."

"What's wrong with me going with you, are you afraid of something?" I shook my head and managed to laugh. "Situation like this is full of tension. I want to handle it myself. Please let me go alone."

She took a sharp look at me. "Okay, be my guest." Moji was silent all through. She knew what it looks like to be confident in someone, but only to be disappointed at the end of the day. Though, she had always trusted in my academic excellence, she knew never to overlook the decision of the WAEC examiners. If history is anything to go by, we have had situations in the past where the best students of St. Jones had often turned out to be the last in their WAEC examinations in the history of the school. So, she wondered what could be her brother's fate as he goes to check his results the next day.

CHAPTER ELEVEN

I sat on that big stone, a little distance from the staff room. There were plenty of ex-students around the noticeboard. It was so crowded that no one had time for another; everyone was searching through the board to find his or her name and the result. We all had a common look on our face at arrival, but soon the expression on student's faces changed. Pophue, Lamid, and Andara were waiting to see their own result too. Everyone knew these guys to be one of the unserious students in my set. They were noted to break school rules and regulations at liberty, and they had been disciplined many times, especially Pophue who derived pleasure from being stubborn in every perspective. He and his crew were well noted for organizing parties in the hostels, or sometimes for inviting female students over to their hostels to take part in grooves. These activities were not acceptable even outside the school premises as per school rules and regulations. It happened several times that Pophue and his gangs were involved in quarrelling and fighting over the school rules and regulations and even causing injuries to others. I was not a friend to these guys; they were too rough for my liking as a person, but all of those things don't matter now. The most surprising thing about them was that girls in the school liked them very much.

They stood around the board with a number of girls making all sorts of jokes, laughing, while other students maintained a steady queue to check their results. One could see the difference between these two emotions: a student in a distinct motion of thoughts over the outcome of their five-year's study in the school, and the later are full of nonchalant attitude toward whatever is the outcome of the result.

Somebody blew a wind into my ear from behind; it was Williams, my old classmate.

"Boy, what are you doing here? Have you checked your result?" he said and walked around to sit beside me. "Man, it's too crowded. Look at them," I pointed. "But sitting like this will not help. It never will stop being crowded. Everyone wants to see their own result. After all, I have seen mine." He smiled happily.

"And what is it?" I questioned anxiously as my face looked somewhat brought over. "Ha! Ha!" He laughed. "Goodies for you, homeboy!"

"How many?"

"Six credits and one pass." He put his hand into his waist pocket and brought a white paper. "Wow," I screamed.

"Also credit in English and Mathematics."

"You are gone man."

"Of course, what do you think?" he replied and continued laughing. "But I saw your sister and your girlfriend in the crowd some moments ago. I think they were helping you out."

"You mean Laura?"

"Yes, together with your sister. They were close to the board when I saw them . . . well, you have nothing to be afraid of, and we all knew you in school that you will pass," he said jokingly.

"And what about you? Aren't you also doing well in the class?" I replied in the same manner. "Boy, never you compare someone who is sleeping with a dead person. It's too different situation." We laughed.

"Who are those two babes walking in our direction?" He changed the topic at once. "Don't tell me you don't know Iluna, Mike's girlfriend," I whispered. "And the other?" he whispered back.

"I don't know her. I guess a friend of her." In a short moment, they were standing before us. She embraced me. "Long time, no see, Senior Basky," she said. "Meet my friend Lena." We shook hands. "And here is my friend, Williams." They exchanged their greetings. "Everyone knows him," Lena said openly while smiling. "He was the literary master."

"Yes, truly you know him," I confirmed.

Williams represented St. Jones in all literary and debating competitions against other schools across the country. He was brilliant and for that he got some level of recognition among students even of other schools and teachers alike. He was known for his eloquence in English language, especially when it comes to analyzing issues.

"Congratulations," Iluna said while smiling. "I am happy for you guys."

"Oh, thank you very much," I replied. "One of the best things that happened to me in my life." Williams looked suspicious. "And

I beg you guys, don't put the rest of us in the dark. I would also like to congratulate somebody too." We laughed.

"Laura and I just did a family introduction. Hopefully, the traditional rights will follow soon."

"Good to hear. Big congratulations to my homeboy," William said. "My guy, you are on the right track to a family life, but I hope you are not compromising your education for this."

"No way, we are not yet married, only to avoid some sneaking around, that's all." Lena came closer to hug me.

"Mike also conveyed his congratulations to you," Iluna said.

"Where is he, checking out his result?" I looked around to catch a glance of him. "No, no. He is in the States."

"What!" I shouted in surprise. "You mean the United States?" She nodded happily.

"He left two months ago. It was a last minute decision by his uncle who visited Nigeria to take him along. So, he had little or no time to inform anybody."

"Anybody, you called me anybody to Mike?"

"No, that's not what I meant." She began to unzip her bag. "This is for you. He sent it by courier." I opened the envelope and read: ". . . knowing fully the kind of relationship we shared from youth, I pray and hope that our mediate family will stick together as one, side by side as we both climb through the height of success and greatness. Would you give my regards to your wife-to-be, Laura? It's so great to hear the news."

"Your friend is now in the United States. What will happen to you and your relationship? How will you cope with the agony of distance?" Williams voiced out to Iluna. "Something will work out soon," she replied, "like traveling to join him?"

"Why not, but not sooner before WAEC?" she admitted.

"But that's next year," I said.

"Trust me, senior, I can manage. It won't take a lifetime."

"And don't forget, guys, she is an American citizen. She holds the passport," Lena snapped.

"I see," Williams said, "that explains the confidence." He nodded his head continuously. "I hope when you are leaving, you will hide me in your luggage. I wish to see America too," I said, and we all laughed. Williams stood up and excused Iluna for a short talk. She stood up to join him, and they walked a distance into the field.

"I like your friend," he uttered without any delay as they walked slowly. "And I want her to be my friend too."

"But she's already your friend. You guys have been talking all these while."

"Spare me those jokes, girl, you know exactly what I meant," he said frankly.

"So, how do I come in here?"

"Good question. She is your friend. You can talk to her for me. She will definitely not refuse you. The fact is that I like her so much."

"You guys, always hunt for girls around."

"Point of correction, baby girl, I am not one of those boys you are talking of. I don't hunt for girls. They hunt for me. I only go for the one I truly desire."

"Okay, okay. I get your message, but my friend is not one-night stand girl, or the type you can break her heart," she said bluntly.

"Now, you are talking. If I was that kind of guy, Mike and Paul would not be my friends. You know, birds of the same feather always flock together."

"You have a sweet mouth," she said. "Well, she has no boyfriend at the moment. She's from a good home. I guess you will find out more about her later. I will do my best for you. Would you come to school tomorrow about this time? Check on us at block C, form four class. I just hope she likes you."

"That depends on you, depends on how you portray me to her." We watched them walk back slowly to the scene.

Moji spotted a glance of us on the field. She and Laura began to make their way on toward our direction. They looked unhappy. "Most people there," Laura pointed, "are so happy with their result. Even Andara of all people got four credits. How does he manage it?"

"That is WAEC for you all," Williams replied. "It gives honor to who does not deserve it."

"What about you, Senior Williams?" Moji questioned. "Six credits." Everyone looked at him with a congratulations look. "But did you find Paul's name on the list?" he asked. "Yes, we did," Laura answered, "but neither subjects nor credits were attached to your name. Some say when that happens, it means your result is withheld or you have something to clear with the school authorities."

"They wrote contact 68011," Moji snapped. "Is he the only person they wrote that on his name space?"

"No, a couple of other names have no results too." "The question is what is 68011?" Williams said slowly to himself and immediately stood to his feet. "I will be coming back soon, guys," he said and began to step out of the field.

On the way, Williams met Tresant. He looked somewhat in a state of panic. "What is it homeboy?" Williams asked. "Come on, you are looking so terrible. Is it about your result?"

"Yes, Williams, I am in hell. I think my result is withheld. They wrote contact 68011, and my aunt is in the car waiting for me. What can I do now, and what am I going to tell her?"

He went on lamenting, swinging his hands. "What is Basky doing there? Has he gotten his own result?" "He has the same problem as you."

"You mean the same 68011?"

"Yes."

"If that is so, I am beginning to get some picture in my mind. I just hope that is the case."

"How do you mean?" Williams asked.

"If somebody like Basky is also referred to that number, maybe it could be a good thing after all."

"I can see some sense in what you are saying. Let's go to the staff room to speak to some of our teachers," Williams suggested. They doubled up to the staff quarters.

Tresant and I were like cat and mouse academically in our school days. We offered almost the same subjects, and we almost have the same approach toward our studies; therefore, many times our results were identical. It made it almost impossible for us to be good friends. We were somehow competitors that refused to give in to the other. Sometimes, I tried to put some extra energy in my class assignments as to have an edge over him but definitely not in Biology. He was simply the wizard, and we all knew of it; he was two steps ahead. Well, I had the edge in physics and chemistry all through the years, and sometimes in Mathematics too. Well, that is how interesting it was in our school days. It is now our history, and we are moving on to other things in life. I think the issue of the 68011 had suddenly brought us together as friends. So, it's another direction of life if I may say we have to find out together what had happened to our results, why other students got theirs and ours not included.

Nearly all the teachers were in the staff room, unlike some occasions where lecturers would be in classes and the staff room would be completely empty. "Yes, what do you want?" Teacher Duroja, the geography master questioned. All students in the school knows him so well for his no-nonsense attitude toward students; he is a very strict teacher to the core. One has to be fully ready to confront him over an issue; he is such a teacher that loves to create problems out of nothing. "I say what do you boys want from us here? I am sure I am speaking a language you all understand, or you don't understand English anymore?"

"Sorry, sir, we are here to find out where the location for 68011 is?" Tresant answered.

"Are you speaking for yourself or the rest of the boys?"

"No, Yes, sir, I mean me and my other friend."

"What do you mean by no? You mean you and your other friend? Then, what are you doing here?" He pointed to Williams. "Disappear from my sight. Where is the other student?"

"He is on the field, sir."

"Doing what? playing? Anyway, the staff room is 68011, so go get your friend to join up immediately. Others are already waiting in the VP office."

"Yes, sir."

Tresant happily step out to join Williams on the way.

"Please do me this favour' Tresant uttered as they walk together, "help me to inform my aunt, she is in a green Toyota car with a plate number: LA 48 kzn at the car park. Inform her of the new development, and that I will join her at home at the closing hour." "Okay, my pleasure" Williams said joyfully with a happy expression on his face. "Thanks a million. I will go and get Basky with me" he said and they started on their separate way.

Teacher Duroja was still standing by the doorway as we walked into the room. He announced our arrival, and everyone stood up in honor of us. The staff room was rearranged to meet up the quality of the occasion. All fifty-two teachers were present, seated beside each other and facing the high table where the government officials and the WAEC members were sitting. The vice principal was also with them on the high table. At the extreme end, opposite the entrance door, were four other students already on a sitting posture. We were directed to join them. What a pleasant surprise, there was television crew and camera crew by the left side of the door! They were filming the occasion for broadcast. It was a day I will never forget in my life; it was happening so fast like a dream.

I began to wish that Mum was here with me to witness this ceremony. She offered to bring me, but I rejected it. My best friends among the teachers—Mr. Waheed Omeza, the Physics teacher, and Mr. Balo, the Chemistry teacher—were smiling all the way through. Then I realized it would be a great memorial day for me and a guarantee to look forward to the future.

Indeed, there is a reward for what everything a man does in life. I confirmed the adage to be true today which marked the end and beginning of a new chapter in my life. Though the occasion was quite new to me, I never had any one spoken about and given such a great recognition for many students together at the same time; this was my first time to witness students who had performed well being honored by WAEC officials for their performances. I knew about making parties by the school authorities in honor of the outgoing students at the end of every school year. We have done that already a week after the WAEC examination.

Come to think of it, none of the students in the school knew what was going on in the staff room; they had made it as secret as possible for a reason best known to them. However, we stood up to the national anthem before the surprise event started.

The VP admin stood up and began to read out from the sheet on his hand. "Members of the ministry of education, the honorable WAEC officials, and my dedicated members of staff allowed me to briefly play around the program of today by expressing my greatest joy of all time, as a proud principal of this beautiful college." He stopped reading from his note to look at everyone with an expression of contentment, and then he continued, "These happened to be one of the finest set of students of this college since 1967. From the beginning of this college, there has never been a performance like this, whereby the best six students in WAEC examination across the whole of West Africa are coming from the same college and the college happens to be St. Jones High school. And to crown it all, I also happen to be the principal of the college at the time of this special occurrence . . ." The teachers stood up and gave a continuous round of applause as the VP continued his speech. "We are not going to waste much of your time, since we have just two hours for this occasioned. You are all welcome to St. Jones high school, Iyatan. The next item on the agenda goes to the WAEC officials." "Thank you very much, Mr. VP," the lady among the four others said as she stood up. One could easily say that she is from South Africa. Her accent easily gave her away, but she was a good communicator in English. She went on, "On behalf of the examination board committee situated in The Gambia, we proudly congratulate this college for such an outstanding and wonderful academic performance of excellence your students had displayed in our last examination. Never has this happened in the history of this WAEC board that after checking our record, making sure we properly control all the results, the six most brilliant students in West Africa happen to come from the same college in Nigeria. A huge surprise it is, but a happy reality. Hence, it explains the reason for this occasion here today. Before we come to the students, we have some gift items." She pointed at them. "We have for . . . ," she looked at the sheet on her hand, "ten of your teachers in this wonderful college who has put in some extra energy on their work, to make this occasion possible through their relentless efforts on their students." The teachers, including Mr. Omeza Duroja and Balo, the Chemistry guru, were all called out by name to receive their gifts.

The lady sat down, and the next official stood up. "Without discipline household, the house will certainly take wrong direction and also wrong decisions, therefore, we also have a special award to the principal on behalf of the council. This token is for the head of the college, Mr. VP Schildra." The ageless school principal, he was about sixty-six years old but still very active on his job. Everyone stood up to the honor of him with applause. The third official stood up to take it over the announcement. "Ladies and gentlemen, with the power invested in me as the secretary general of the examination council, I wish to invite each of these students forward to collect their result, and a token amount attached accordingly." He took a deep breath. "They will be called out according to the numbers of distinction they scored. The last three names are third, second, and first. That means these three students have the highest distinction in their nine subjects and very identical result."

The first student called was a lady, a brilliant lady, who had come to retake her examinations, but this time around, she took all the glory. I was the second to the last that was called by the official. The lady had so much experience taking WAEC, so she probably had no reason not to do well this time around. So, with her brilliancy and previous experience, the sky became no limit for her to fly on.

Tresant was among the first three students; in fact, the best among them. He scored six distinctions including Biology and three other subjects.

The staff room had suddenly become a fun center with applause and laughter everywhere. Everyone, both old and young, was enjoying the fun of this great result for the college. The WAEC officer again glanced on the sheet in his hand and called my name, just as he did to the others; I stood up and remained in front of my seat. Everyone gave a round of applause with good cheers.

"Paul Basky," he repeated and looked at me. "We congratulate you for your hard work and your good performance in this examination, and we further wish you success in your future endeavors. You have scored a total of eight distinctions and a C4 in English language, making you the second best student in the whole of West Africa." Everyone rose to their feet to show some appreciation with happy gears. I felt so much joy and satisfaction within me, after all my effort has paid off. The officer proceeded with a little biography of me from form 1 in St. Jones, my character, academic performances, and my relationships with my teachers. "Therefore, with the result you have achieved before us today, any institution around the World would be most glad to have you study in their university and of course in any discipline of your choice too. It is an envious result of the highest standard. According to what we have been informed by your college principal, your area of interest is to become an engineer." A whole lot of gear took over again. He drank from his glass of water for a short pulse.

"Well, this is a great day for you, son. We wish you a continuous success as you proceed on in life. On behalf of the examination council, in addition to your good result, we are also presenting you with a cash gift of 50,000 thousand naira." "This amount is to go into your academic pursuit for the future," Mr. Omeza, the Physics master, shouted the loudest as he was overwhelmed with the gift. "We would share it together," he said, and everyone laughed over it again. He is my best friend among the tutors in the college. He is a man who does not only see himself as a teacher, but also as a big brother to all his students who knows what they wanted. He protected me, gave advice, and corrected me too; in fact, he helped me with the selection of my final year subjects when I doubted whether to do all science or a mixture of arts and sciences. I liked his subject the best. Therefore, though I have the right to reserve the points for myself, all salutation and regards can only go to no one but him, Mr. Waheed Omeza, who started his teaching carrier at the Government Day Secondary school, Okekere, Ilorin, Kwara state before he was transferred to our college. I was very privileged to have him as one of my special teachers. I miss him.

Nefi was also called out for a honor. She was the number one student in West Africa for this year. Something very strange about her was that despite the way everyone was shouting to honor her achievement, nothing seemed to amuse her. One could tell out rightly from her unique attitude, she felt it is just normal. She collected her result with a cash prize of 100 thousand naira.

The VP stood up. "The next agenda goes to the representatives from the ministry of education in Lagos." "Thank you very much," the middle-aged man said as he stood up with a dominating smile. "I sincerely thank everyone for making this occasion a commendable one, especially the students who are the brain behind this occasion. In my opinion, there is no need to analyze any geographical location and all that as much had been said and done here today already," he smiled. "Despite all that have been mentioned, it will be incomplete if the ministry do not officiate the new road in which these children will continue to their various destination. We have seen many brilliant students in the past, but they eventually hit a stumbling block because of lack of proper guidance for their future, and many of them were not able to accomplish their full potentials and that is very sad if they have performed very well in their final secondary school examinations. That is why we would not only stop with the cash prizes given to them, but we would go further in the realization of their academic pursuit." The entire room was silent. Everyone was listening attentively to the end of his productive speech. "So in the light of the above, the Federal government has awarded scholarships to the students, to study in any Federal university of their choice and also the first course of their choice. Once they make their choice, our ministry would arrange the admission for them and prepare them to join the new school academic year." He stopped and made some whispering discussion with some of his colleagues with him. "From every perspective," he went further, "St. Jones high school is a great college that deserved an upgrading to a college of excellence. From the ministry and my colleagues here, I present this official record to your college as institute of excellence." He walked out of his chair to lift up a round beautiful portrait and hand it over to the VP admin. "It is recorded officially in the book of history that St. Jones is merited as the best secondary institution in the country. The award will only shift from your college when another college is able to get your present record of success. We congratulate you sir for such an outstanding achievement under your leadership." The VP raised the portrait up for everyone to see and admire, and the teachers were very joyous, while everyone stood up as we clapped our hands to the happy merriment of the day. The man stood up again. "The first three students with the highest number of distinction will be sponsored to a higher institution abroad to complete their chosen carrier, so they could choose to study in Nigeria or travel abroad for the studies, but the decision would be left to the students to decide. Details of the arrangement will be sent to your VP at a later date. And the rest would be admitted under the same study program here in Nigeria with a monthly allowance of 40,000 thousand naira. Details of these arrangements would also be forwarded to your VP. Sorry, I mean your former VP." Everyone laughed but wondered what he meant by that comment.

It was a great moment; there is no doubt about it. We were glad to witness a day like this. It was once in a lifetime, a day that proclaimed another phase of my destiny to begin in a different world, a major part of my story that formed the meaning of my title. "Thanks to God almighty for giving me a day like this," I said to myself silently as I joined others to walk out of the room. A small group had gathered at the door to the staff room, following the events of things that happened inside the staff room. I came out to the embrace of Laura and Moji outside the staff room. "Girls, I have enough story to tell you guys," I double whispered alongside to both of them.

Chapter Twelve

Believe me, words are not enough to describe the joy in our home. I became the focus of all attraction in the house. Everything I did or said found its comfort in everyone's mind. Moji and I had now become closer than ever before. She had begun to believe so much in me, both as her elder brother and as one whose future was in my hands. She had begun to count on my judgment toward her studies, believing the fact that I could help her secure positive results in her coming examination.

It was already two weeks since we had that occasion in the staff room in my former school. As usual, in the house, we had just completed our morning prayers. Laura had also spent the night in our house, so we had the morning prayers together that fateful morning. "I duly thank God for your life, my son," Papa said as he stood up to address us.

Mama also joined him, standing and looking at each and every one of us.

"Everybody sit down. I have something interesting to say to you all." He had a happy expression on his face. I looked at Laura's face too, and she smiled back at me in response. Moji moved closer to Mama and held her hands tightly.

"Go on, sweetheart, we're all ears," Mama said happily. "Well, before I go on to say anything, I like to thank all of you for the love and respect you show to one another. Your prayers for me as head of this family have come to pass and it has continued to yield good results." He looked at me. "Paul, come here." I walked to him. "You have made this family very proud. Not only that, you have also made me a proud father. I am very happy with you in all regards. Thank you, son. The other day, I promised to reward you with something special. Huh, you have not only achieved the medal but also added a multiple diamond to prove yourself capable of keeping your promise. Here comes my own promise. I have opened a new bank account at First Bank PLC on your name with a deposit amount of 500,000 thousand naira to appreciate your success in this family and for a job well done. Here is your passbook." Everyone shouted happily.

"Why are you crying, Moji?" Papa asked in a soft voice. "I am just being happy for my brother," she replied.

"Your time will come, my daughter. I know you are like him too. Your time will come soon, my dear," Mama said and rubbed her head. I went on my knees. "Thank you very much, Papa. I guess I never would've made it in the first place without all your support at all time when I needed it. You have given us love and preached confidence into me. Even when I got no point at all in my test, you still treated me like a king who has won the whole world. When the issue of Laura and I happened, both of you stood out and showed us so much love as parents. I count on your continued support, sir. Some families would have fallen apart in a similar situation like this. Instead, you made it very easy for us to move on. So Papa, what you have just given to me is not a token, it is a fatherly blessing from a good heart, and you have continued to do this since my birth. May the good Lord continue to bless you and mama always. May all good attraction continue to be the foundation of the Basky family."

Everyone screamed, "Amen. Amen." "I still have good news for you all," Papa said. He stood up and walked to the dining table and unlocked his brief case. A large envelope was in his hand. "Guys," he raised the envelope up, "this is the result of hard work. Paul, you have been awarded a scholarship to study in Maclodia University in Munich, Germany, to a Master- degree level. This is wonderful." Everyone including Mama rushed over to embrace me for the good news.

It is no surprise, Laura had just begun to cry. There was no amount of words that could dry up the tears. "I will go with him," her voice mingled with her cry. "I don't know if that is possible, my angel, but we would find a way round it. Trust me, dear, we would surely do. Stop crying," Mama replied in the same tone. She covered her face in the hollow of her laps and went on crying.

Having seen the emotional condition of Laura, Papa invited me into his study room to inform me about my departure date and all necessary arrangement made already by the ministry of education.

"My son, are you very sure that your decision on this boy is correct?" Grandpa asked Papa in his usual low tone. "Because I see him as too young to go abroad all by himself. He still needs parental guidance. So, how can you decide so easily on a fragile issue like this, throwing him to the white people's world without any person to help him with the decisions that he has to take over there?"

Papa smiled. "Have you forgotten?" Papa asked. "Forgotten what?" Grandpa asked him back. "That God has a purpose for everything that happens in the life of a man."

"Are you telling me what I taught you?" Grandpa said. "Well, since you know this very well, you should as well know that a mortal's mission and time in life is being controlled by the only great Master who does it better than what we think." "What does that got to do with the age difference I mentioned of?"

"Papa, yes, indeed Paul is your grandson as we both know, but I can assure you, he is no longer the little boy you think he is. He is twenty-one years old, but with a matured mind of a man over forty. I have been studying him like a book, and he has grown and matured that I have confidence to release him to the world. He would be fine, Papa. I saw the strength of his capabilities. If not for that conviction I have on him, I would've rejected the offer in the strongest terms that he travels abroad. But fortunately, that isn't the case at this point. You know me, Papa. You know how much this two children mean to me. They are all I got. So, I must be careful in the decision I make for them."

"Paul," Grandpa called my attention, "are you ready to travel abroad, away from your own people?"

"More than willing, Grandpa. It is for my education purpose, and it would expose me to more knowledge and understanding on how things work elsewhere. I will get to know the world better, so I think, Grandpa, I am ready for it. I hope to learn other cultures and make it useful to my life's development. Grandpa, I understand what your worries are, but all protection comes from God almighty alone. I hope to go there with my two eyes open and be the useful one you expect me to be."

"If that is what you want, you have my blessings. But don't forget all your promises. Don't forget the principle of the Onigba spirits binding you and Laura. Do not cast it aside because you think you are in a different world. Huh,", he shook his head in wondrous manner, "I guess my word should be enough for you if you are truly my son."

"May the will of God be done in my life. I will keep all promises as long as breath is in me. I pray my partner will do the same."

"Yes," Grandpa said, "keeping your promise will do us much good. I wish you a successful year ahead out there."

"Thank you, Grandpa, I will always need your prayers."

In no time, all conversation came to an end. Papa still had a long journey to make, though it was already 14:00 p.m. midday, but still he wanted to make it back to his destination. He dropped me at home and began his journey to Lagos.

CHAPTER THIRTEEN

I was lying on my bed, tired from the whole day's event. I tried to listen to the night news on television. Laura came out of the bathroom, having taken a shower, and she just turned off the television without informing me. I know she got something on her mind she wants to tell me. We stared at each other for a minute, and we lusted for each other. You can see a deep sexual look on her like wanting me to touch her. Who else will not, not after seeing such a straight and beautiful body of hers? She was young and fresh. Her nipples have the power to turn anyone on. She was a girl of 1.70 meters tall, light in completion, and a pointed nose. All these values added to her charming beauty. I stood up to reach for her, but she simply refused and still stood by the television, looking directly in my eyes. What I saw in her was a stare of worries, concerns, and insecurity, a selfless confidence that has no other choice than to agree with the majority. To her, leaving her behind was like losing her love to the European sharks that awaits me over there. I stood up once again and drew her closer to me and held her close to my chest; she pulled off and she went to lie down on the bed, but she turned her back toward me, again the tears came flowing back. I rubbed my hands across her breast and turned her to face me. She responded.

"Make love to me, my dear. Let me have the very best of you, who knows it may be our last time together, since we have chosen to live apart in a different world."

"What do you mean by that?" I raised my head to look at her. "Don't make it look like this is the end of the road for us. I am not the first person in this town to travel abroad for further studies. Neither would I be the last. I just don't see how this would bring us apart. After all, I have the plan to bring you to join me in a short distance time when I finish my studies." Her face brightened. "Are you sure of what you are saying?"

"Have I ever given you a promise that I never kept to date?" she broadened her face with smile. She then moved closer to me and held my chest tightly, using her stiff hard breast to feel my body. We began to kiss, fighting all through with our tongues. She was a passionate kisser; she tried to leave a lasting memory with me. She put her hands into my pants and began to play with my thing again. She stroked my penis up and down, making it to become as hard as a rock. I made love to her again, and this time around, she really felt me and enjoyed it. I tried not to make it painful, so I did it carefully. We did it like it was our last time, but at the end, we both were tired and fell asleep.

The next morning, I saw a different Laura. She acted to love me more than before. I thought it could have been the sexual intercourse we had the previous night. I did not disappoint her. I was proud of myself too, at least I could satisfy her and leave her with fun memories of me. I hoped that would last her till I come for her when I finish my studies in a couple of years. I checked the time. It was 12:20 pm. Although we had a great time together, but it was late for us to get up. Through all of these sexual contacts, we regularly used protection after the first garden experience. We agreed to protect each other from any form of disease or unwanted pregnancy. What a pity, but it is for our own good.

Frankfurt Germany

Chapter Fourteen

y journey was quite fun and comfortable. It took us about six hours fifteen minutes to cover the distance of Lagos to Frankfurt. It was in the month of November, a period of winter in Europe, a period when the weather is never friendly at all to anybody. One can imagine how cold inside the aircraft could be, but arriving in the country became another hell of cold. The difference was like a man brought from a hot Sahara temperature to a cold atmosphere where the natives are no exception to the cold condition. Imagine what that looks like, my friend.

"How are you, sir, welcome to Frankfurt," the German immigration woman said. "Is this your first time in Germany?"

"Yes, please."

"And if I may ask, what is your mission to Germany?"

"I am a student. I mean . . . ," she interrupted, "you are a student from Nigeria. What does that got to do with your mission to Germany?" She was very serious with her line of questions, and her look did not make matters easier for me, but I just wonder what her problem is.

"You are not getting it." "Make me get it then," she snapped. "I have an admission to Maclodia University in Munich." I unzipped my handbag and brought out my well-arranged documents and gave it to her. She glanced through the documents and then pressed a button on her cabin. In five seconds, two healthy tall policemen walked straight to her. She gave them the documents including my passport. With their gesture, I followed them to a nearby office. They were friendly, but it's an opportunity to dig into one's privacy as to help get rid of that person, if he has not genuine purpose to be in Germany so I could not kind on their kindness as policemen. "Have a seat, please," One of them said. They withdrew into the inner office to engage in some discussion as they kept on checking through all my documents, and they made a phone call.

"Thank you for your time," one of them said with a brief smile. He gave my documents back to me. "You are welcome to Bundesrepublik. We hope you will have a good time with your studies here in Germany. We are going to bring you to your flight gate to Munich. Please come with us." I took the flight at 13:15 p.m. to Munich. It lasted only forty-five minutes of what I called a satisfactory journey.

There was no much ceremony as they have it at the International airport in Frankfurt. The local airport in Munich was simple and nice. Movements around the airport were not restricted whatsoever, as there was no immigration control, except for the Customs whose duty was only to check any suspected passenger's luggage. The good news was that I was left to a free passage at the arrival hall where many were waiting for families and friends. My concern was how to make it to the University according to the direction given to me by the ministry of education in Lagos. It is a foreign land, not always easy for an alien, especially for the first time visitor like me. I dragged on my bags, just a few distance from the exit door when I had the announcement on the air, "Mr. Paul Basky from Nigeria via Frankfurt, please proceed to the information desk c at the arrival hall."

A young beautiful white girl with blonde hair was standing beside the desk, holding a plank on her right hand. A sign of frustration was written all over her face. I thought that wasn't my problem. "May I help you, sir?" the fat woman in the desk said in a friendly tone. "Yes, you called my name on the air wave moment ago." "And what's your name, sir?" "Basky. Paul Basky," the blonde girl beside me raised her head at once. "She is waiting for you." She pointed at her. "Hello, Paul", she said. Her mood brightened up. "My name is Bettina, and I volunteered to pick you up to the campus. I am also a student of Maclodia." She collected one of my bags, and we began to walk through the exit to the car park. "How do you get to know of me, I mean of my arrival today? By the way, it takes a big heart to come and receive someone you don't know or you have never seen before," I said admirably. She laughed. We sat in her car, a BMW, and she drove out of the airport into the free highway. "Every international student's arrival date is always published on the noticeboard, weeks before departure from their native country, and for you," she looked at me and smiled, "I made it a challenge to help you out."

"Thank you. Thank you, Miss . . ." "Bettina," she helped out. "Are you a German?" I asked as she drove on. She shook her head. "No. I'm Swedish, from Stockholm. Do I look a German?"

"I don't know. How do I know how a German looks like?" She nodded her head. "You are right," she admitted and smiled. She always smiled to everything I said so far. She looked simple and easy to talk to. "I thought German was supposed to be the only language here. People speak English fluently all the way through."

"Don't even go there," she said and turned into another street. "You are now in Bayern, a place where English is like a poison to them. So, you have a lot of learning to do." "But everyone has been talking to me in English, and what's the difference between German and Bayern anyway?" "Bayern is one of the regions in Germany. The Bayern people are known as the Bayerish. You will learn about the regions that make up Germany in your language studies, but start getting it in your mind, English is not the language here in this country. Airport is a general place for all people, so they speak English, since you have entered into the country, it is all German. So, expect it to be the national lingua for everyone here. Don't mixed up, you will soon know it." I began to think of how to live in such a country as this where they speak no English at all. She noticed my worries and interrupted my thoughts, "Of course, don't worry, Paul. Everything is going to be just fine. There are other foreign students including me, and we shall be your friend soon and will make it comfortable for you."

"But how would I communicate with other people?"

"I know that's what you are thinking," she said and smiled. "You will undergo a German course, intensive program for one year before starting your full course."

"One year?"

"Yes, and it depends on every individual. Some people go on as far as two or more years, while others achieved it in less than eight months. So, it all depends on how fast you are willing to adapt and learn the language."

"What about you? How many years did it take you to learn German?"

"No years at all. I was born here, so I know the language from birth."

"Good for you. What level are you now in the university?"

"Two. I still have five years to go before graduation. Then another two years in Hamburg school of medicine."

"Oh, you are into sciences?" I questioned interestingly.

"Yes. I hope to be a medical practitioner some day. What about you? What are you aiming at?"

"A civil engineer!"

"That's great. Germany is definitely the place for you. They are the best."

"Guess what," she said, "my friends would like to meet you. You are so nice to talk to. Your girl must be proud of you."

"Well, thanks to you, Betty," I replied, and we kept the silence all the way through the ride to meet her friends as she dropped me at the campus. We arrived at the student hostel at the main campus, known as Studenten heim. The buildings were structured in a modern architectural design: a well-mounted skyscraper that gives uniqueness to its kind, the flowers around the premises were indeed done by German specialists in a way of modern technology, according to human mind of beauty. "Jump out, guy," she said happily. "Welcome, home!"

"Where is this?"

"Registration office, you will be registered for an apartment here." Both inside and out of the building was jam-packed with students from various countries, everyone trying to secure their own accommodation.

"Can you speak German?" the young man said in a funny gesture to me. "I wish I could," I replied. "Don't worry. We would also register you for a language lesson now. Your passport please," he requested and went further. "Here in Germany, we call people by their surname. So, don't be surprised about that," he said while writing some information on my passport. "Please go into that machine," he pointed to the room, "I must take a photo of you." I obeyed. "Take these forms and answer the questions on them. Make sure you return them tomorrow before 10:00 a.m. You are on a scholarship from Nigeria, so all payments have been taken care of. Those forms in your hands are very important. Keep them well and return them back to us like I said earlier by tomorrow morning. Your monthly payment will take effect from next month if you return those papers in your hands for official use." He opened a big safer box on the wall. "This is your keys, and your apartment is in Panke house, Zimmer 164. I think your friend knows where it is located." He looked at her to ascertain, and she nodded her head. "You are lucky to be in Panke. Your country specifically demanded for the best for you. I wonder why." He looked at me with a note of surprise, so does Bettina. "These are the rules and regulations of Panke. Study them at your free time." I collected the booklet, and we stepped out of the building.

There had been a lot of ups and down in München. The language program had not been easy to match up, but I did my best. Despite its intensiveness and my complete devotion, I still found it quite rough to climb through the stair. Many students said I was trying though, but I wouldn't say much on that because I know it is not the standard yet to reckon with at this point.

I was walking across the field to the other side of the language hall where I was to catch up with a lesson. I saw Bettina and two of her friends walking toward my direction. "Hi, Paul, meet my friends, Kerstin and Rachel." They smiled. "Pleasant to meet you guys," I said warmly. "You are a fresh student," Kerstin said in a friendly voice. "When I see a new student, I know one." "Don't spell too far," Bettina fast-forwarded. "I told you already that he's a new student, so don't give us those . . ." She went closer and closed her mouth with her little finger. "Well, a formal introduction is needed at this point," Rachel said in a low key tone. "And that should begin with you," I said. She smiled. "Everyone knows my name already. I'm from Augsburg and a student of Microbiology. I live off campus." The two others clapped their hands jokingly. "My name is Kerstin as you already know. People call me Keestro, the fun babe, guess why, because I am among of those few that makes it happen in the campus. I would stop at nothing to catch my fun always and . . ." "Huh, lady Keestro . . ." the girls snapped, shouting in praise on her. "Don't mind them," she said and went on. "I'm from Nurnberg, and a student of civil engineering, part two. I reside in Panke house." She raised her hands up in cheer victory. I took a second look at her. "She is my course mate and also resides in Panke. I guess she will be a great value to me," I said to myself.

"Okay, Betty is the next person," I said. "No, no. You're the next," the two girls shouted jokingly. "We know everything about her already. We also know that she is the Münster of Maclodia." We laughed. "Okay, okay. Call me Paul if you want, or my surname, Basky if it pleases you . . ." Kerstin interrupted. "Can we sit under that tree there?" she pointed. We agreed and began to walk toward the direction. She held my hand on her left hand as we walked, slowing to take our sit.

I wasn't comfortable with her holding my hand, but I said nothing. I know I must be diplomatic before I become the cause of trouble for three female friends on campus. I am still new here. She sat closely beside me, so close that Bettina began to notice something about her behavior. "Okay, girls, as I said earlier on, I am from Nigeria, somewhere in the area of mid-western region in Nigeria. I am from a family of four, my parents and a sister. Can I say something, please?"

"Go on," Kerstin answered as she placed her left hand on my lap. "I need to meet up with my lesson now. It's about to start."

"Don't worry. I will teach you German. I will make you speak it so well."

"That's thoughtful of you, but I need to go now." I stood up to start moving.

"Oh, before I forget, Paul," Bettina snapped, "would you please join us on Saturday to Flash Night? We shall be going in company of other friends."

"Where is Flash Night?"

"It is a special discotheque in the city. Please don't say no," Kerstin said. "Trust me, the groove would be a living memory." I laughed. "Well, be my guest."

She rushed up to give me a peck on my cheek. "You are just too cool," she uttered. Rachel and Bettina began to look at us wondering. We exchanged greetings and started on our direction.

CHAPTER FIFTEEN

enis Mayer was a student I duly respect. He was a man well guided by principles and he acted in maturity. I guess it was because of his age difference. He decided to go back to school, to obtain a degree in Economics.

"What do you think of here?" Denis enquired, a soft smile went through his face as he waited to get my answer. "Captivating," I replied, "nothing irresponsible about it, I like it here." We sat around a big table, a distance from the dancing floor, beside a drinking bar. "This is Flash Night. There is no two of its kind here in Munich. That is why it is located in Karlsplatz," Liber voiced, a close friend of Denis whom we occupied a table together. "But what do you mean? What's special about Karlsplatz?" I questioned.

"A lot of things makes it special, my friend. For generations, the Mayor of Munich declared this area to be an historical place. Mr. Karl was said to be a great man who brought lots of fame to the people of Munich, and I mean the Bayerish. That is why the government honored him with such important recognition in the society."

"Okay, I understand that," I forwarded, "what exactly had he done to merit the recognition?" Denis shook his head to my question. "Discrimination was the authority of the day here in Munich in those days. He was the man that fought over it, a battle that he sacrificed his life and that of his generation. It was so terrible, but he had to do it for the sake of the future generation. If not for him, other races would not have come to live here today." "Indeed, it is outstanding," I admitted. "That is why any outlet that is to operate in this area is properly checked and with no discrimination intent," he concluded.

"I see, that's why people are so friendly out here," I whispered to myself.

Liber sat beside his girlfriend, Ankar, a blonde beautiful girl from Hamburg. Kerstin and Rachel went to buy some drinks for everyone. Bettina sat next to Denis.

The club was indeed a place of fun. Many young boys and girls occupied the whole vicinity enjoying themselves. Most of them were dancing, adding to the value of the night. The music was an old school-type; they never fade away. The DJ was an American, African-American from the State of Alabama. Although I never had any contact with him whatsoever, from my observation, he seemed to be the model everyone was looking for in a club like this. Most people, including myself, never stopped wondering on how well he did the mixing so perfectly that he created uniqueness out of what he does. From what I later heard about him, he was the leading DJ in Munich.

"Guys," Kerstin said from a distance as they approached our table. "I ordered the same drink for everyone. Nobody is to drink something different from the other," she said and began to drop them on the table.

"But how can you decide on people's choice?" Denis said as he took a closer look on the drinks. "Paul doesn't take alcohol. He requested for malt." "Yes, I know, but he has to learn just the way he's doing with his German." She looked at me and smiled. It wasn't funny. I call it stupidity. "I will give you the best treat of your life tonight. There is much fun you don't know about here in München. Trust me, I will lead you there," Kerstin said with smile, as she swung her body to the ongoing music. "But that doesn't change the fact that what you ordered is not what I like to drink" I said being serious.

"I never take alcohol my whole life, and I don't intend to start now." She stopped dancing, stared at me with her eyes blinking. "Am so sorry," she said and began to cry. She sat on the vacant seat beside me, and buried her head on my shoulder.

Everyone looked at one another and fell somewhat dumbfounded. "Obviously, there is more to this," Bettina said and shook her head. She began to open the drinks for us. "Should I open this for you?" I shook my head, meaning no. Kerstin stood up stubbornly and opened the beer that was meant for me. She seemed so determined to do something which I was not able to figure out. Ankar and her boyfriend stood up immediately and walked to the dancing floor, leaving the rest of us behind to settle our differences. Denis was also not happy about the development; he stood up at once and lost into the crowd. She ignored them all and concentrated on me. "Am sorry," she said, "don't mind my attitude or what I said. There is a reason for it."

"And what could that childish reason possibly be?" Bettina said annoyingly. "Bet, I will appreciate if you don't intrude in my privacy," Kerstin replied with a serious tone.

"Do I hear you say privacy?" Kerstin stood up on her furiously, but I stopped her from getting closer. "What are all these supposed to mean? We came here to have a nice time, and you guys are destroying the fun for everybody. Sit down, Kerstin. Don't allow any stupid tension come over you." She refused. "Let me talk to her skull. Among everyone here, she knows how best to insult me, the wise one of all."

"There you go again," Bettina replied. "You have really gone beyond what I thought you are. You know what, a child will not act as cheap as you are doing tonight. Get this into your filthy head. If I've wanted him all these while, he would've been mine before you even know him. I drove him in my car from the airport to the campus. He is my friend and would stay so, nothing anyone can do about that, neither you nor anyone else. Okay?"

She stood up and asked Rachel to go to another table. I was angry, and stomped my fit on the ground. "You send everybody away. Tell me, what's your stress, girl?"

"You are my stress, baby."

"What do you mean?" I looked at her eyes.

"I am really going crazy for you. How can I make you see it? Something terrible is burning inside of me for you. I may be acting silly before everyone. It's the passion for you that is driving me insane. I never meant to offend anyone, but not to worry, they are my friends. I know how to handle them. All I need from you now is to get me out of my confusion."

"In what way?"

"By holding me close to you and telling me that you love me."

"No, that cannot be! I will never tell you that, and honestly, I can't love another woman. I have a fiancée back in Nigeria. You don't even know me and you say you love me. Sorry, I've not told you about her, but there is no reason for that anyway. I don't have to discuss her with you." She looked frightened and somehow confused with my answer, but this is the truth. "Fiancée, Bettina, or who?" A shrill of violent tone began to appear on her voice like she was ready to fight that person. "I am talking of my woman back home in Nigeria. Her name is Laura. Please get me right, she is not any person here. I am just here for few weeks now. I am not interested in any lady here, please."

"Why did you keep such information away from me all these while? When you introduced yourself the other day, you made no mention of any woman in your life. Now that I have you in my mind, so deep a feeling, then you are telling me all this."

"I am sorry. Please understand and bear with me." "Understand me too," she shouted. "Whoever you claimed to be your woman is in Africa. I am here with you. Let her be for you over there, and I am for you here in Munich." Tears were rolling down her cheeks. "I wish it is as easy as you say it. Unfortunately, I cannot cheat on her. Just as I know she will do no such thing to me."

The music on the air took over the airwaves; it was a slow sound track, another track from late Marvin Gaye's "Sexual Healing." Bettina walked in and invited me for a dance. I was glad she did, thanks to her for bailing me out of this dilemma with this lady who does not understand what I am saying to her.

"I don't know what you guys are up to, but I just got to give you my best shot. She isn't that kind of girl you may think she is," Bettina said as we held close to each other to the effect of the rhythm on the dance floor. "She is a go-getter. Every girl knows her in the school. She always wants every new international male student to warm her bed and dump him after the experience. She is not in love with you but to have you, so you better be careful with her. Remember, she once told you that she will stop at nothing to get what she wants. So be wise."

"Thank you, Betty, you remain my best friend." I replied.

"Take a quick look at them, Paul, that is Ugine," she said on my left ear as we matched along with the music. "Who is he?"

"Ugine is the son of Menco Achman, one of the top politicians in Nurnberg. He is the only child and very rich guy."

"Why is he coming here so late?"

"This is one of his club investments."

"Flash Night?" I looked at her face in surprise. "Yes, of course," she admitted. "He is in the company of four men and two girls."

Guess what, Kerstin never stopped amusing me. She rushed up from her table and ran joyfully to embrace him. They had several mouth kisses, something very intensive. It puzzled me toward who Kerstin really is.

CHAPTER SIXTEEN

*U*gin's house was situated at the heart of Olympia centrum in Munich. It was a mansion, quite a fortune, an action figure that could make anyone to look at its direction. What often captured my glance each time around was the custom-built swimming pool that was erected at the front of the castle, giving it a resemblance with the White House in Washington. There is nothing to manage about the land where it is built, quite spacious and accommodating for hundreds of guests. The entrance gate was noble enough to be compared to a president's home. Well, whatever my description may seem like, all I mean to say is that his house does have many interesting elements to write a whole pages about.

"I even heard from a source that his girl would be coming soon," Rachel said. "Who?" Kerstin questioned and answered by herself out of anger. "The so-called Laura he is talking about?"

"Yes."

Rachel replied with a wicked smile. They sat in Ugin's master bedroom. "Is it about that African girl you told me of?" Ugin asked. He reseated uprightly on his king-size bed in his room. "Yes, the girl I told you about. He made her a saint," Kerstin replied angrily. "Then we shall see what to do about her. When would she be in town?" he questioned. "Still on process I think," Rachel replied and moved closer to him on the bed. She placed her head on his chest and reached out for his pants. He was a Casanova; every girl liked him for his money. He was a lavish spender and a sex maniac. Kerstin also moved closer to them, and they started with all night long sex affairs.

Let me update you with the progress of my education so far in Germany. Besides the one-year language program I was engaged in, I had spent two years of my five years course, and I am doing my third year in level three hundred at the university.

My German skills in writing, reading, and speaking had now improved to a professional level. I could communicate in simple German language and write it. I could also read very well. I no longer have any problem with communication as it was in the past.

Thanks to the world of Internet that makes it much easier for me to play around with gathering information and searching out things myself without depending on any person.

I now had people around me I can truly call friends, someone like Denis Mayer who had proven beyond doubt that he is genuine, good, and kind hearted. He had been there for me in times of dark clouds and challenges. What about Bettina Scorn? I never knew a white girl could be this good as she was always there for me as a true friend. Many students rumored we were involved in a secret love affairs, but there is no truth in it. She was just a good friend unlike her other friends who were just interested in sleeping around for money.

Rachel was a close friend of Bettina. They shared many secrets and good ideas together, but of late, there was someone around not saying the truth, so they seemed not to trust each other again as before.

It had been four years and two months since I left Nigeria for Bundesrepublik, Germany. My only means of communication with home had been through letters, and sometimes by phone when I had the chance to use the public phone and there was connect back at home in Nigeria. I missed my dad and mom very much as well as my younger sister, Moji, and I also missed Grandpa. Moji and I had been communicating via writing. I still miss her though. Saying that I miss Laura is an understatement; I was dying to see her. I had been waiting for the day of our reunion, never to part again till we are separated by death.

That day, the 15 November marked one year and twenty-six days since I started the process of getting a visa for Laura to join me in Europe. Now it's over, a confirmation was sent to me by my dad that she got the visa and she would be arriving soon. Papa gave me her arrival date, so I need to arrange to receive her. Everyone, including Kerstin, had volunteered to come along with me to the airport to welcome her.

Although Kerstin's offer did not go down well with me, I could not refuse. They all seemed to be happy for me. I wasn't sure if her coming with us meant any good or to cause trouble. Well, I had to pick up courage and allow fate be my advocate.

I got Laura on the phone to talk about her coming to Germany. We were all excited about her coming over. The next time we spoke, she was calling me from Germany itself.

"Darling, I can't wait to see you," Laura said on phone, calling from Frankfort airport, as she was awaiting a connecting flight to Munich. "We shall be there by 10:00 a.m."

"How is everyone back home?"

"They are fine and getting younger. I have plenty stories for you tonight. Don't leave the airport sweetheart . . ." she said and the phone suddenly cut off. I lost contact with her, but I knew I will see her soon.

All my colleagues made a banner, and they carried it with them to the airport. The banner read, "Laura you are welcome to Germany." Denis and three other friends of his also came to join us at the airport. Libber was the good guy that assisted me on how to make all procedures on enrolment possible for Laura. Without prejudice, he deserved whole lots of compliments.

She was the sixth passenger to come out of the custom check, at around 9:48 a.m., a beautiful moment to behold forever. I ran toward her as soon as I spotted her and lifted her off her feet, and she was hanging in the air. She wrapped her hands and legs around me and buried her head in the right part of my neck. They made a circle around us, clapping their hands with laughter on their faces and cheering us on.

"Thank you very much, my love," she said in a low key tone in my right ear. "You said it, and you kept your promise." A mole of tears began to roll down her cheeks. They were tears of joy and celebration.

None of them understood what we have been passing through emotionally, it has been over four years since I left her behind with a promise to come for her.

"These are all my friends, Laura. We are in the same university. They are all good guys." She started from Libber and went through everyone giving them a handshake. "They are the people that make life comfortable for me here." Bettina brought out a special flower and poetry she has written on her behalf and gave it to Laura. Kerstin also brought a long beautiful flower and gave it to her too.

Denis made it more than I expected. A group of Bayerish traditional singers were invited by him, and they suddenly came out from nowhere and began to play a special welcome number for her. She was pleased beyond her wildest dreams. Happiness was verbally written all over her face. It took no training to see through her mind on how much she felt blessed that she is being treated like a queen from a special Island. Under Libber's request, we moved to a metropolitan snack bar at the arrival hall area where he had made a reservation for us all. We continued the merriment there all at his expense.

"She is not looking ugly," Rachel whispered to Kerstin. "She looks like a model and wild lady, exposed to life in Nigeria. I see why he has gone for no one else here."

"Who cares, there are so many tasteful menus around the world," Kerstin said. "If I gam I refused to eat from Ugim I, we have a way of making others share the plat with ega—min," she replied in the same low tone, a typical Bayerish slogan in the act of evil. "What are you having in mind?" Rachel questioned. "I hope you don't do anything stupid."

"You wait and see. I never demand payment from you in order to see, do I?"

The melodious effect of the music was beginning to storm the entire arrival hall. People had now gathered around the scene to take part in the exercise that was full of fun. The Bayern people loved their cultural music, so it was no surprise to see them gathered in large numbers, holding each other's hands and swinging their legs to the effect of the chorus. "I told you, I never like that girl," Denis said behind my ear.

"Kerstin?"

"No. Rachel. She is a corny fox. She pretends to be a good girl, but her heart is full of evil. Don't you see them gossiping all these while as everyone is having fun here? They are up to something else."

"I need to use the restroom," Laura said slowly in my ear apparently standing up from her seat.

"Let me walk her to the area. She is new here," Bettina replied with smile. So they vanished into the toilet area. "Are you a German too?" she asked as they walked back from the toilet.

"No, I am Swedish, from Stockholm. I guess you are from Nigeria too."

"Yes, of course."

"You will also need to go through a German studies class like your man did before you begin your course. Your guy is now a master in the language, so he will also teach you some from the very beginning."

"That's great. He will be my translator for now." "Of course, as you wish," Bettina replied jokingly.

"I am really going to deal with her this time," Kerstin said to Rachel as she saw them walking back to the midst. "I don't know how she does it. She has a way of bringing people close to herself." "But Betty is one of us," Rachel uttered.

"I don't care. The more I look at her, and the closer I see my plans coming to past."

Laura was laughing so loud like a loose monkey from a zoo. She was like being let out to reclaim her long-lost treasure that had been missing for so long. They sat beside each other, and the conversation between them was flowing like they had known each other for years. Laura was likeable to people and very friendly. I could see an icon of understanding developing between them, just as it was with me.

Libber had a lecture to attend by 3:00 p.m., so we need to be on our way out of the airport. It had been a fun afternoon for us. He drove across the autobahn, and in a short while, we were back at the campus.

I still remember what Laura said at a glance of Panke house. It is definitely not easy for a newcomer to accept Panke as a student hostel. It is like a five-star hotel and definitely well equipped.

CHAPTER SEVENTEEN

"Call me names if you want, I want you to give it to me like the old days," Laura said. It was 10:00 p.m.

We were hungry for each other, terribly in need of one another. Apart from missing each other for over four years, the condition was conducive for us to do whatever we want to do. I had an apartment to myself, and we were all by ourselves for the first time with no interference from any family member. We took our shower together that evening and retired to bed around 10:00 p.m. We spent most part of the night on lovemaking till we had no more energy left to continue, but we started all over again in the early hours of the morning, and that was great fun to always be remembered. As weak as I was, I took my bath, dressed up, and stepped out for my daily lectures.

It had been one year since Laura arrived from Nigeria to Germany. She had been working so hard with the language program which was to end in the next four months. Though she had not been doing so well lately, worst of all, she had been very muddy, keeping to herself these days. It's been going on for some time now. She did not tell me what was the problem with her, and I could not adduce any reason for her change of attitude and behavior. I decided to wait and hold on until she opens up to me again. I sat on a stool beside the flower pot, watching her reading a text book. She had been silent the whole day, not still talking to me what was bothering her. I was determined to put a stop to this silence that day; no matter what it was, she must talk to me.

"I believe I have some right to share whatever is your worry, my dear. You don't need to go through it all by yourself, please."

"What do you want to hear from me?" she burst out angrily at me. I had never seen her in such a mood in my life. I stood up and walked to her. "I knew there must be something on your mind, because you have never behaved this way since we knew each other. Whatever it is, it must be very serious to make you keep away from me all these days." I looked into her eyes.

"After you are done and repented, you then decided to bring me your old fool from Nigeria," she said angrily at me. "What is the meaning of this Laura? What have I done to you?" It was beginning to make sense to me now; someone had been feeding her with stories which were not true about me.

She did not talk again. She stood up and went into the living room. I walked behind her still wanting explanation on her comments. She was definitely upset, but I don't know why.

Suddenly someone was at the door knocking; she quickly put herself together and went to unlock the door.

Bettina was there, and she came in with her usual smile to chat with Laura.

"There she is again," Laura said embarrassingly to her. "Haven't you had enough of him? Are you not ashamed of stealing someone else's man? Are you not?"

Bettina was shocked at this reaction toward her, and her mood changed. She couldn't imagine such utterances coming from Laura that she had accepted as a good friend. She stood dumbfounded by the doorway, unable to say a word; neither could she advance further inside the apartment.

"What did I had you say, Laura?" I asked angrily. "I see, now I got you right. That has been the meaning of all those immature behavior you have been putting up all this while. Who has been feeding you with these malicious accusations?" I moved closer to her. "What have I really done to deserve this kind of insult and wrong attitude from you, Laura?"

Bettina, with little tears in her eyes, said, "I am not that kind of person who goes out with any type of man without looking into what future such relationship would be. I have my own man if that interests you to know." She showed her finger toward us. "And does this make any meaning to you? This is my wedding ring. My husband is a medical doctor in Stockholm. He is working at one of the biggest hospitals in Sweden. My interest in Paul is to help him have a good stay in the university and enjoy his studies, the same friendship I extended to you when you arrived in the country. So I will advise you to look vividly into those accusations of yours before drawing a conclusion on what is not true and ruining your relationship. I am not interested, and I am not in a relationship with your man."

"I may have come from Nigeria, but that does not make me stupid. I have come across people like you before, no wonder you chose to be so close to me as a friend. You think that will help you to cover up the secret of your affairs with Paul?" She shook her head. "I don't think so." "What proof do you have on this allegation?" I questioned her angrily.

"Plenty, as much as you want," she replied. She went into the bedroom, came out with an envelope, and dropped it on the table. "And these are some of them." They were photographs, pictures of Bettina and me at Flash night, holding each other while dancing. Also at a swimming pool in Odeonsplatz, and some other places over the years. I never realised Laura was that kind of extra maniac in an act of jealousy. Of course, I know we all do one way or the other, to protect our beloved one from losing him or her to an invaders. Unfortunately, it is only few of us that use our head and not emotion to put things right. And such people of patience are those who win the battle at the end. "This is a big set up," I shouted. "The motives you have in mind about these pictures are not true. Don't allow these pictures to deceive your thoughts. People are working on you to destroy us." I walked closer to her, apparently to touch her.

"Take your hand off me," she pleaded and she stepped backward. "I find it very difficult to believe you again. That means . . ."

"That means what?" I interrupted, "Have you forgotten so soon, the Onigba in Iyatan, at least if not for any other reason, with the park alone you should always trust me. Bettina has only been a good friend. These pictures," I lifted them up, "was in Flash night. The first time I just arrived in München. You can ask Rachel and others." She smiled, like making a mockery of me.

"Yes, Iyatan, but 'Onigba' could not stop you or harm you when you crossed the line, flirting with other girls."

"That is because I never crossed any line. Can't you understand this? I am only telling you the truth here, my baby. Nothing but the truth." A load of tears began to track down on her cheeks.

"Paul, I am disappointed," she said. She walked into the bedroom and collected some of her text books. Without further delay, she marched up to the doorway and stopped beside Bettina. "I will never forgive you. I never knew you are my enemy," she said and walked out of the apartment, leaving us speechless at the door.

"I am very sorry, Bettina. I am really and truly sorry for all of these embarrassments. I will get to the bottom of it." She stood motionless on the spot. "I knew where this came from. I knew who is beating this dirty drum, but I never realized they will wait these long before they strike at me. I should have told her about Kerstin, about all her advancement towards me. I should have done so."

"Kerstin?" A sharp look dropped on her face. "Yes, Kerstin and Rachel. I never trusted them, and I knew they were up to nothing good but evil. Now, look at what they have started."

"Oh my God!" she said and placed her hands on her head. She walked quietly out of my apartment.

CHAPTER EIGHTEEN

*R*achel loved her apartment very much, a self-contained apartment in Trecher strasse in the heart of München. It is a hostel for students who wish not to live within the campus, especially those who could not afford to pay for the accommodation in the campus, or those that just want to be left free to do their own thing without anyone questioning them.

Most of those unserious students find it very interesting to hang around such places to make their unholy deals. Trecher area has been noted by the police as crime-infected area, and students living there are warned to be careful at all time.

The vicinity has a bad name, both for the students' community and the university.

They sat freely on the rug in the room. No chairs were available, not even a stool. Visitors always made themselves comfortable by sitting on the Turkish-designed rug that beautified the room. A twenty-four-inch television set and a CD loader sound system were placed on the floor. There were four large pillows scattered around to help out when seated on the floor to provide comfort.

A number of ashtrays were lying at every corner of the room for an easy reach for smokers. Three bottle of champagne were already opened as they were busy entertaining themselves. They looked happy and smiling as they drank and smoked. Playing on the background was an old Eddy Grant music, and they were busy on a discussion.

"I don't know who the hell he thinks I am. Cheating on me is like taking away my soul. I will not take that from him. I am not going back to him," Laura said.

"Did you tell him who informed you of all his secrets?" Kerstin questioned as she pumped in a smoke of marijuana. "Of course not, what do you think, a baby? But I showed them the pictures."

"And how did that stupid girl reacted when you knocked the nails on her dull head?" Rachel asked eagerly. "What else do you expect? She was dumbfounded, of course." She drank her champagne.

"I tried to stop them, you know," Kerstin lied, "but Bettina confesses about how good he is on bed, that it will be difficult for any woman to let go easily. Considering the fact that he already told us about you when he arrived in München."

"Well," Rachel said, "that's life. She saw an opportunity, and she grabbed it. It can happen to anyone else."

"Yes, just as it's about to be my turn," Laura said angrily. "No, don't be stupid," Kerstin mucked. "What about the ritual affairs way back home?"

"To hell with whatever they called those rituals, if he can do it and get away with it so freely, why can't I?" She sipped some drinks from her glass. She had began to look tipsy, but carried on stubbornly drinking. I knew her too well. She was not the alcoholic type, a mummy's pet and princess that was been followed around by royal guards in Iyatan, such person cannot be good in reckless life. What an irony of life! Well, this is Europe as they often say, a place where most Africans think they can change their good moral way of life to another culture of misbehavior. Most of them use such opportunity to emulate bad habits in the name of civilization. They give no more regards to moral discipline, goodness toward God and man.

She regained her balance on the pillow and began to dose off slowly again. Kerstin and Rachel quickly passed on a glance at one another and began to smile at achieving their wicked act. They felt satisfied with the direction things were going. They planned all of this, and they obtained the expected result. Therefore, Kerstin brought out a pack of cigarette, and with some marijuana, she began to roll them together, lit the wrap, and gave it to Laura.

"No, no, I am not good at this at all."

"There is always a first time to try something new. Try it, baby. Just a puff is enough for you. You don't need to swallow it. Just a pull and pour it out. It will make you feel real good and relaxed. You will enjoy it with the wine. It is a perfect combination."

She stretched it toward her again. "Yes, try it, girl," Rachel supported, nodding her head.

"No, please," Laura said, "this is a line I don't want to cross no matter what Paul has done to me. I don't like smoking, and it is nothing for me. So I will appreciate if you let it be." She sipped the champagne again and swung her head to the music. The house bell rang from downstairs, and Rachel pressed the intercom to open the door. A tall, good-looking gentleman came in, putting on a white complete suit and a white shoe to match. Also, on his head was a cowboy's hat, a designer combination. On one of his fingers on his right hand was a good-looking ring that could win anyone's mind, and what an expensive watch on his left hand. Despite the cloud of smoke that gathered around the room, the fragrance on his body dominated the whole place with a good smell for any woman to notice and give attention.

The three ladies quickly stood up and embraced him one after the other. Laura felt so impressed with what she saw, handsome-looking guy. The other friends noticed her look on the man, so they felt she could be swept off her feet easily with this good look. Deep inside her, she was already feeling something special for him at a glance. "Laura," Kerstin said in excitement, "this is my friend. His name is Ugine." He stepped closer and kissed her on her cheeks. "Nice to meet you, Ugine," she replied.

"Well," Kerstin went on, "Ugine is a millionaire with lots of cash to spend on his friends. His dad is a well-know politician controlling the affairs of this country. He owns most discotheques in town, like the famous Piccalady, B.A disco, Flash Night, and many other establishments."

"Really?" she said. Kerstin nodded yes. He smiled. "Well, splendid to meet you," she admitted. "What are you girls doing at home? Why not we go to Piccalady for some fun tonight? We could have a nice time out there you know."

"Why not?" Laura replied.

"Okay, let's do that," Rachel said and withdrew quickly into the bath for a shower. Kerstin also joined her, living Laura and Ugine in the room. He sat on the rug and rested his back on the pillow. Laura sat at the opposite direction, looking not comfortable with him alone.

"Has anyone ever told you how beautiful you are, very attractive like a model?"

"Yes, all the time, my mother and my lover."

"Yes, they are right. I see you as all men's choice. No man can resist your charm."

He tried to touch her, but she avoided him.

"Sorry about that, but truly I can't resist a beautiful woman like you. I am immediately falling in for you," he said as he rebalanced himself on the pillow.

"But you are Kerstin's boy friend," Laura said. Looking surprise. "Says who? We are just friends, nothing special about us. I take care of her and help her with her needs. She is not my girlfriend except if you want to be mine, our relationship will be very romantic."

"Well, I don't know you. For now, please keep a distance from me. Will you?"

"Yes, I will," he replied.

Although Laura said so, but she could not keep her eyes away from him. Deep inside her, she could not help thinking of what could happen to her if the spirit of the Onigba were real as they warned, but come to look at it from a different side of view, if only Paul did what they claimed he did, it means there was no reason for alarm over the identity of the so-called Onigba spirit, she assured herself.

The girls had their bath together. Of course, they were lesbians and bisexuals. They have no regards for men whatsoever. They had spent some memorable time masturbating one another; being the plan they had in place for Ugine to get over Laura's mind, just to break the bond between her and Paul. And so far they were on track; everything seemed to be working perfectly for them as planned. So, what an achievement to jubilate about, so they stayed put in the shower to enjoy their evil act.

Ugine's limo was indeed a different one. Laura was carried away with what she saw. What else could one have expected from a high school girl, passing through a Western lifestyle of glamour and riches for the first time? I just could not risk believing that it was my Laura I am talking about, dropping so fast without looking behind to review the past stories between us. She was prepared to throw everything to the wind for the new, wild lifestyle of her newfound friends.

She was the only black girl in the midst, and was been treated like a queen.

She sat beside him, while others sat opposite them in the limo, enjoying the music as it played, and they drove off to one of his popular joints in the city.

Piccalady is not a discotheque. It is a bar with a sitting hall, classic for meetings and relaxation, a beautiful joint. It is situated somewhere in Schwarbben, along Leopoldstrasse, a distance from Münchner Freiheit. It is a place where stars from around the world often come to relax when they visit Germany.

It is a well known place in town. Piccalady is not meant for everyone; in fact, certain class of people are not allowed in, except if they are women accompanying members to the place. So people are restricted to visit the joint, except with a membership card of such, but never easy to get one. Women, of course, are always welcomed to Piccalady. They are the first priority to a free entrance if need be. even if she comes with a man. They attract these rich and famous men to the joint, good business for the management, that is piccalady for you.

"Everyone respect him so much here," Laura complimented pleasantly and smiling to her friends. They sat on one of the VIP tables. Ugine was busy talking to one of the guest customers beside him. "I told you," Kerstin whispered to Laura, "he owned this place. What do you expect from people who work for him? Of course to respect their boss." One of the servicemen walked down to their table to take their orders. "You know what," Rachel said in a low voice, "I could see Ugine's interest in you. I think he likes you."

"Exactly what I'm afraid of. He is Kerstin's boyfriend. How do you expect me to friend the same man with my friend?" "You are wrong. He is not my guy," Kerstin interrupted, "he is just a friend of my boyfriend. How can you expect me to go out with my lover's friend? It is not honest to do that." She lied.

"Your boyfriend, how come I've never met him? And you also never mentioned him to me in all our discussions, not even once?"

"Because you never asked me, have you?"

"Girls, what is important now is what to do with Ugine," Rachel quickly intruded, "as we can all see he wants Laura. I could notice that in the limo."

"I don't think I want a new relationship for now. I will like to take some space out to get myself together and get over Paul."

"This is an opportunity for you now. Don't be stupid about it. It is only a chance, and if you don't take it, it may not come back again. Not after what Paul did to you before you came here. I see it as an opportunity to grab real cash to move on," Rachel said frankly.

A dose of confusion stared on Laura's face. She became silent thinking about what direction to follow, but it took her no time to make up her mind.

"I can see you girls are doing just fine as I wanted. Why don't you ask for more things?" Ugine interrupted and pressed the bell on the desk. A waiter quickly appeared to take new order. "Bring more champagne, chickens, and whatever they want to entertain them. They are my guest tonight. Write it on my bill, Okay?"

"Right," the waiter assured.

He withdrew to get their orders again.

Ugine had a conference to attend on Monday at 10:30 a.m. in Düsseldorf. He wanted Laura to accompany him on the trip, so they had to leave Piccalady soonest so that she can have a good night's rest having had much to drink. Laura spent the night with Ugine at his mansion home, while Kerstin and Rachel were dropped off by one of Ugine's friends at the joint. Hard to believe, Ugine made love to Laura that night. He was a champion in doing what women like most in lovemaking. So, he did all he could to win her heart, and he seemed to have succeeded. "Yes, I have taken the right decision," Laura said satisfactorily in her mind as she laid beside him on his king-size water bed in Olympia Centrum.

Chapter Nineteen

"How old is she?" the polizei questioned. "Twenty-one, sir, she left home since Friday, after a brief misunderstanding, and today is Wednesday, still no trace of her." He was busy typing out my statement on a PC as I spoke. "Was there any serious confrontation between both of you?"

"Not really, we only had some minor argument."

"Argument as in what form?"

"A little quarrel like any among lovers, nothing unusual."

"Okay, your passport or ID please?"

I reached to my jacket and gave him my resident card. "Thank you," he said and withdrew into an inner office. "I don't like these people," Denis whispered. "They are simply a trouble diggers, looking for people's fault at all time. He's going to check if you have been booked for any crime or such."

"He can even go beyond that. I don't care. I am clean." We watched him walk back to us. He gave the ID card back to me.

"And what now?" I asked. "Mister, the law says you must wait for another two days for her to return, but if it exceeds two days after you made this report, then we would step in fully and make it a missing person's case. The good thing is that you have come to report her to us that she is missing. We have it in the central system now, and wherever the police find her, we will bring her back home. Here is a copy of your report." He gave me three documents. "But this is strange. Maybe something terrible has happened to her somewhere and yet you ask me to wait for two more days before they can commence action on a report case of a missing person." I shook my head in disbelief. "She is an adult not a child. No matter what, she still holds the right to her privacy. I repeat, the law says two days, no more, no less. Good day, gentlemen," he said and watched us walk away in an unfriendly manner. Denis tapped my shoulder, and we stepped out of the Praesidium to Schafhofstrasse. "No surprise about that. This is their way of operations here," Denis said. We made a sharp turn to the quiet street of Bayerbrunner. "I will simply advice you to be patient about the whole episode. Something tells me your innocence will be proven somehow, but not to do anything stupid before then. I understand how you feel."

"Please, can we sit down here for a moment?" I requested. We sat on one of the chairs meant for the Heineken store arranged along the roadside. "A medium-size glass beer will do for me," Denis answered the waitress. "And you, sir?"

"Water, please."

"Can I ask you a question, Paul?" I looked at him, meaning yes. "Are you guys already married back home?"

"You wouldn't understand it all, Denis. It's a bit complicated than what you think. There is something traditional attached to our relationship. I guess you will not understand no matter how I try to explain it to you."

"Make me see what you mean then," he said anxiously.

"Unfortunately, it is not a subject I want to talk about at this moment, please. I am sorry. I would prefer to skip this discussions to another time when I am in a better mood to talk about it."

"Okay, if that will bring my old Paul to life." He smiled. The waitress brought our orders and left us alone. "When have you seen Bettina last?"

"About the same day I saw Laura last. I think she's not happy with me. I just find it difficult to see my fault in all of this."

"I am quite sure, Kerstin is behind this entire problem," he said. "One of those pictures was snapped the first night we visited Flash Night with you. Remember, it was the same night she tried to propose friendship to you. I saw her when she took those snaps."

"You saw her doing it and you hold your peace?" I raised my head toward him. "Slow down, I never knew she has any wrong intention for taking the pictures. You know me too well. I will never support anything evil, never to encourage one to do a thing like that," he said. "Well, the damage has been done. Her purpose has been achieved," I said effortlessly. His phone rang. "What's up, guy?" he answered Rolland. "Quite some fun out here," Rolland replied.

"Where are you?" Denis asked. "At the English garden having a cool nice time with friends. You are missing out."

"I am somewhere in the city with Paul."

"I tried to reach him already, but his phone is switched off. I saw his girlfriend with some guys here in the garden. I think she must be drunk." "Who?" Denis asked curiously. "Laura, of course, that African girl. Are you out of your mind? What is the problem?" Roland questioned in a surprising tone. I collected the phone. "Hi, this is Paul." "Hi, Paul, why did you switched off your phone? Your girl is out here in the garden. Why are you not with her?"

"Okay, which location are you?" Tension grew up from my voice. "Are you coming?"

"Yes, we are, but do me a favor. Please don't tell her I am coming. Where are you precisely?"

"Join up from the direction of Leopoldstrasse and ask for the Irish pop. You can't miss it. You are going to love it here."

"Stay around, friend, we are on our way soon."

"Any time for you guys," he said and he hung the phone.

Change, change is one of the meanings of existence. Everything, including man, rotates along with time. It is very painful when a loved one is suddenly thrown into another phrase of living, another chapter of time, making the past uncompleted history that never stop killing the mind. It is a bitter reality anyway; I have not stopped shedding tears due to what fellow men did out of hatred in order to achieve good things of life. It means changing a true destiny that is meant to be. I saw it coming, but what can a man do without God almighty, I guess nothing?

"Don't do something stupid when you see her. It will not make things better," Denis said as we approached the Irish pop. A live band was playing. That was why the area was jam-packed with people. Phil-Collins was the guy in question, doing what he does best in entertainment world, bringing males and females together to grease the lover's day. We stood by the large entrance door. "I still didn't see them," I said, following the loud noise coming from the dance hall.

"Okay, let's call Roland," he suggested. "Are you guys here now?" he asked. "Okay, wait by the entrance. I will be there in two minutes," he assured.

Dorothy ran over and gave us a peck. "Rolland and I have been waiting for you guys, what's up?" she said while smiling. "We are good," I replied. She is Rolland's faithful girlfriend. They have been together ever before I came to Germany. They operate a distance love affair because of her work in Aachen. Therefore, she is no friend to any of those bad girls around in München. "You are not looking cheerful." Rolland suspected at once. "What is the matter?"

"Laura," I replied. He pointed in the direction of the stage, expressionlessly on his face with surprise. "She is over there, in the midst of Ugine and his friends. Oh, now I get the picture." He shook his head.

I shouldn't have done that, I know. Tears were tracking down my face. Dorothy quickly walked closer to me, and placed her head on my shoulder to comfort me. "Don't do that, Paul, you are a man." Roland placed his hand at my back. "Whatever is the problem between you two, she definitely doesn't deserve a good person like you . . . I know you so well. Most girls will love to pay so much to have you with them." He squeezed my shoulder. "I suggest we leave here now," Denis said. "Let her follow the direction she chooses for herself."

"No, I can't," I uttered. "I need to have a glance of her, even if that will be for the last time."

"Okay!" they agreed together.

The path that led to the hall was so tiny and crowded. People were standing at all parts of the way, grooving and enjoying themselves, but despite the busy atmosphere, we began to walk slowly in between the people to make way for us. As I made my way through the crowd, I was confident, very sure, that she would come back to me if she set her eyes on me because of what we both shared together. We have destiny written in our palms together, and we cannot allow it to fade away.

"That's her," Dorothy pointed. "I asked of you from her twenty minutes ago and she responded quite well." She was in the company of Kerstin and Ugine and other big boys in town. I guess one of those in the corridors of power. Their moods were nothing but that of fun. They cared about nothing at this point in time. They were just having fun, while I had been suffering alone. Laura was really doing so well in their midst, just having fun like nothing happened. I still don't have the idea how so fast she had been incorporated into their evil and ugly lifestyle. She was sitting on Ugine's lap holding a glass of beer in her left hand, kissing and laughing at the same time with all affection. She seemed to be in great satisfaction. I couldn't believe what I was seeing, and thank God, I was seeing it with my own eyes.

"Trust me, guys," Denis broke the silence in a state of tension. "I can feel something not right here. We should just go away as soon as possible, please," he said. "I sense something terrible about to happen."

"I am not going to leave yet," I said in German.

"I have to say good-bye to her. I am not going to cause any trouble here, but she needs to know I was here and I am saying good-bye to her."

"No, no, please listen to the voice," Dorothy said while pulling my hand back. "Those guys around him can be dangerous. They only need a command to turn this whole place upside down."

"They could get away with anything here in Germany. They control the security operatives too," Roland added. "Well, good friends," I said, "I was not born to be a coward. Let my inner self be my judge. Someday, I will live to tell my story." I began to walk toward them in boldness to the front role where it all happened.

Well, what should I say, a man must always accept the challenges of life as a responsibility one has to face each time it comes, neither can a man run away from his own shadow. I will take responsibility over my action. I guess that is a real man.

I know it was dangerous though, but to what extent was what I don't know, but I can't just walk away like a coward without voicing out what was on my mind.

I was determined to carry out this mission, to take both of us back home, back to where we came from and to do what ever necessary to get out of this bondage that brought my life into shamble.

I stood in front of Ugine and his clowns as they lavished their money and rapped in fun. It was quite unexpected of them; I stood there with my hands folded together, looking languorously at her, and passing on a message to her with my look, like saying time is up. "That's him. That's him," Ugine shouted at once, pointing at me. "Get him out of here and put him where he belongs."

A host of men, tall and lanky, about eight of them, rushed over and threw me to the floor, a fight ensued, but they overpowered me. A handcuff was trapped on my hands behind my back, making it very painful as they pulled me up. They were from the police (Polizei). They were not in uniform. They were special protection guards for big boys in society who can pay extra for their services, and these officers were guarding Ugine, his big boys, and my supposed wife. Others in the party hall started screening loud: "What has he done! What has he done! Let him go. He has done nothing. Let him go." Some others were shouting, "Stupid African! Stupid black monkey! Take him back to Africa, back to the forest." Just about the same time, Laura suddenly fell down on the floor, and she began to shake all through like someone having an attack of convulsion. In that state of confusion, someone called for the ambulance. Within few minutes, the ambulance service staff were on the scene, and she was given first-aid treatment before she was moved to the central hospital in Bayerbruner. I was taken in to the polizei headquarter in Plara where I was locked up for their own good because I was alleged to have caused distortion of peace and order in a public gathering.

CHAPTER TWENTY

Who says there is no power in the hands of men? people are capable of doing so many things to achieve their goal, especially when they have the privilege of money and fame around them. "Don't ask question" is the logo. "Do what I say" is the verdict.

The lies that was framed against me was such that was unbeatable. It initially seemed like a joke, but it soon became a reality in my own very eyes. I was charged to court, and the judge, after listening to their lies, went on to make the statement, "After all facts and proofs visible before me today, before this honorable court, you are hereby sentenced to six years in prison, and thereafter, be deported back to your country of origin."

Those were well-packaged lies that I was not given the chance to defend myself, but I was judged based on the lies presented before the court. I was declared guilty of all charges leveled against me. I was accused of causing bodily injury to fun-seeking people at a public place. Also, I was accused of attacking them without provocation. These were all lies. The question was could it be wrong for asking for what rightfully belonged to me, or because I stood in front of them unharmed and unable to fight for my God-given rights? Well, the question was no longer relevant at this point. I was going to jail for no offense at all.

Actually I was later informed that my thinking was wrong. I was not convicted because of what happened in the party event rather for a strange offense that I knew nothing about. I was accused that I was a drug dealer distributing drugs to party events in Germany; I had suddenly become a drug dealer in the court. This was the name given to me in order to make me a scapegoat to cover up the real truth of the matter. They had it perfectly arranged to convince the judge that I was a drug dealer. Who can blame them after all; it's my entire fault, fighting for a cause I believed in, but how will I ever clear my name from this mess? Life went on.

I laid down on that small bed assigned to me in the prison cell at Stagmanda, probably one of the toughest jails in Germany. I still remember how many times people die in a month as a result of constant torture under maximum lockup environment. The only meaningful way to survive Stagmanda for a longer time was to be obedient and serve under the rules of the guards. A prisoner that tries to prove smart or tries to talk logic of any kind can be rest assured of not returning home to join his or her families.

People committed suicide just out of boredom of the environment, and the mental torture was used to break down people's will. Why? Because the biantas (Warders) always have a way of roping people into deeper offenses as far as the prison is concerned. Trust me; you wouldn't want to experience these situations. If they don't like you, you are in trouble, or you try to make their job difficult.

"You have a visitor," a voice announced from the overhead intercoms in my small cell that had become my room for the next six years. It was from the central office of the Biantas. "Dress up in two minutes," the voice ordered.

I had no panic any longer. I was getting used to the environment unlike when I first arrived, and everything was strange and irritating then. I had spent over one year and nine months. it has of course being a living hell in pains and tears, so there is nothing too hard now to bear with my situation. I was getting used to the conditions and situations here; I had learned to obey their rules and regulations and to be patient as the only way to counter their evil plans to frustrate me even more. I had always believed that everything in life that has a beginning must surely have an end; I also knew that my life had a purpose and that purpose will be fulfilled at the end of this ordeal.

Grandpa had died during my incarceration; in fact, six months in to my prison term, the letter came to me, but I could not do anything about it. To be in a prison is a taboo to the elders in Iyatan. It's a big disgrace to the family where such person came from, so I was sure my family had not told anyone of my situation yet.

"I told you never to allowed him go. I told you. I told you." That was Grandpa's last statement to Papa on his sick bed at the hospital in Iyatan. I never will forget him; he showed me so much love and teachings about life that I would never forget him. May his gentle soul rest in eternal peace of the Lord.

In less than one minute, the giant door was thrown open in a loud manner as usual. I stood up and joined the two biantas by the doorway. "I like him," one of them whispered to the other in German as they walked behind me along the wide corridor. "Yeah,

we all noticed him. We may have to recommend him to the judge,"
he replied. We passed through many iron doors across the prison
cells to the other side of the building. It was a well-built maximum
detention center, so the idea of escape was not possible. In fact, don't
even think about it; it is a waste of time and energy. It's a perfect wall
of protection with many modern security gadgets to detect any plan
of escape; there are surveillance cameras into the cell rooms.

Another big door went open again, and I was asked to sit down
on a stool chair by a table. The door was locked behind, leaving me
to wonder who my visitor was. In less than ten minutes of trauma,
two gentlemen in black suit came in. My instant observation was
correct. These men must have brought me some good news, but I
don't know what to expect. For the first time since I am lavishing
in this jail without any hope, God seemed to have finally heard my
cry for help, or maybe it was just my imaginations again. I saw it in
the first glance of them. The look on their faces was not ordinary;
they could not hide the truth away from me. I was only wondering
why it took that long for God to be glorified and his name blessed.

"We are from the justice department," one of them said. "We
came from Berlin to analyze your case, and we discovered some
irregularities in your case, so we came to talk with you."

"What is there to talk about me? I have spent one year and nine
months for an offense I never committed. So why now to analyze the
case?" I asked. "Take it easy, young man," the man with a curly hair
replied immediately, "something unusual is happening in your case.
We have the conviction that there are issues about your file that has
been covered or not clear to our understanding, and beside, we also
came across a report that was filed by you to the police, about your
missing woman on the same day you were arrested. That is why we

are soliciting for your cooperation to see the truth and get justice for you." "And if the truth is finally unveiled and I am proved not to be guilty and innocent, what are you going to do about it?" "We are sure to compensate you for your time wasted," the other man said. "Then, go on with your questions," I said. "Thank you, Mr. Basky," the man with a curly hair said. Both of them unzipped their bags and brought out their laptops, and they began to connect them. "We like to take your permission to record this conversation for record purposes," the man with a curly hair said. They both stared at me for a reply. I nodded my head in acceptance. The other person brought out the recording tape and set it on the table.

"Do you know Mr. Dennis Mayer and Miss Bettina Scorn?" The man in spectacle asked.

"They are my friends. My friends since I arrived in this country."

"How would you describe their relationship with you? Positive, very positive, or negative, very negative."

"Very positive," I replied.

"If you have to compare these two with Miss Kerstin and other friends of yours, how will you describe them?"

"The difference is too clear, sir. They are not in the same category. Kerstin is a very negative person. In fact, her negativity contributed to my being locked up here for no offense." They both glanced at each other quietly and went on, "We have received twelve pages of petition on your behalf jointly signed by Denis and Bettina over your case. And quite interestingly, bringing into account some kind of spiritualism of such," the man with a curly hair said, "does that mean anything to you?"

"Well, yes," I replied. "Okay, please go on."

"Before I proceed on, sir, may I ask a question please?"

"Right, go ahead," the man with a curly hair replied.

"I never spoke of a concept of such spiritual matters with my friends. How come you question me about it?"

"You are very intelligent I must confess, and I duly appreciate that. As a matter of fact, we did not mentioned anyone's name on that. A strange accident occurred, which claims the life of only one person among four people in such a fatal accident as that. It was the same period we also received the petition from your friends. Somehow, it proclaims spirituality in the way we viewed it all. And interestingly, the victim in the accident was mentioned in the petition we received. Hence, brought your matter into serious consideration," the man with a curly hair explained.

"Listen to this, Mr. Basky. We are not here to exchange words with you. We have a mission to accomplish, and that mission is to prove the certainty of your innocence in this case you have been convicted for. So, you better cooperate with us to make the investigation smoother and your name can be cleared on time and you get out of this jail environment."

"Furthermore," he went on, "Ugine had a car accident a week ago, and he lost his life in that tragedy. He made some confession before he died that connects to you, and I hope the story is getting clearer to you now. Do you want to cooperate with us and answer our questions?" Knowing well that whatever I say will throw more light on this matter, there was tears in my eyes, and the tears freely rolled down my cheeks as I tried to compose myself to tell them my little secret which I had kept to myself till this day. I had to tell it to these two strangers what started back in my hometown; the truth has to be told to clear the situation that the police and the justice system don't know about.

CHAPTER TWENTY-ONE

"Well, call it anything you want, it's all about love, about two teenage persons that mistakenly bonded themselves into a living world of mystery. My father once called it a ghetto of mystery. Now, I know what he meant. Now I know that what an elder sees while sitting, a child cannot see it even if he climbs the tallest tree on earth because it is about the age and experience of life." I noticed they were in total attention to my story and curious to know the outcome. They were full of attention and interest. I went on, "There is much to say about my story, but it started at a park in my hometown called the 'Onigba Park' in Iyatan. A male and female from different background and different parents are not allowed to visit there, except if they are prepared to honor and tie the knot of marital values and commitment for life. Laura and I were these two young persons that found themselves in this ghetto of love. We were no longer allowed to choose a different partner in life except in death. The Onigba is ruled by the underworld spirit of love, a jealous goddess that do not forgive when you break that commitment of vow to one another. And to avoid mistake on my part, I did everything possible to bring Laura to join me in Germany, but only for her to break the vows so soon, by joining wrong friendship, and she began to experience a different lifestyle of alcohol, cigarette, and sex. This type of lifestyle is in contradiction to the spirit of our ancestors that watch over us. She was misled to fall in love with Ugine under a disguise of lies from Kerstin and others who helped her to execute this evil plans including lies against my person."

"Is that what you think led to Ugine's death?" the man in spectacles asked.

"Well, such fact would need to be proven. I know what you are thinking, but this is the truth and what the gods of my ancestors have predetermined. I have no reason to ascertain that claim though." "Apart from Ugine, three others are fighting for their lives in the hospital as we speak to you. They have been hospitalized long before the accident that killed Ugine. So what is the connection with the three ladies in the hospital. The strange thing is that clinically, they are well according to the doctors, but they continue to rust in their body, complaining of inner pains," the man in spectacles explained in frustration.

"They are swollen like a time bomb, waiting to explode," the curly haired man added with the same look.

"Who are these people?" I asked.

"Laura, Kerstin, and Rachel. Perhaps you can help out to reclaim back their health by forgiving their fault," the curly haired man requested. "What do you mean, sir?" I questioned suspiciously.

"What does forgiveness has to do with their sickness? I didn't make them sick, so how can I have the solution to their sickness?"

"We understand beyond your explanation, Mr. Basky," the curly haired man said. "It's a simple mechanism. With the story you have related to us about your town and the gods, anyone can see the connection between you and these three persons in the hospital. We are certain at this point that your innocence is not to be doubted. I mean we understand that from what you have told us and from what others including Ugine narrated before he died. At this point, first thing first, whichever way we can, we have to rescue these three persons from dying, and you have to help us, even if we have to plead to the spirits of those gods in your town. This is the time to act, please, so tell us what we need to do because we don't have much time in our hands."

I was short of words. The truth was that I don't even know how to appeal to the goddess. I was only told the implication in case such a thing happens, but I was not told the remedy to it. All these were narrated to me by the Olu of Iyatan. I had never spoken to a goddess before, neither had I seen one before. So, I was as confused as they were on what to do in this matter. Perhaps, even more, but if it is mere forgiveness that would solve the whole problem, believe me, I had already done so long before now. What would I gain to see people lose their lives for a mere mistake that could happen to anyone, not even to talk of my love that I pledged to live the rest of my life with. I had used the period in prison to reflect on this matter and let go by forgiving Laura and the rest. The only thing I was interested was to have my name cleared.

Everyone was silent, unable to choose the next word. They were staring at me as if I was the cause of this current situation; in fact, I am also a victim of it all. They want to hear me speak, to come up with a solution that could cure the ladies, and I didn't have it.

"Okay," the curly haired man broke the silence, raising his middle finger in demonstration, "you will have to come with us to the hospital. Maybe that will do some good." He pressed the button on the table to get the attention of the warders. Two of them came in to join us. "From this moment on," the man who was wearing spectacle said in German, "we want you to prepare his release papers according to the orders of the court."

He handed them a paper which I suspect to be an injunction from the court to release me. "Am I a free man again?" I asked. "Yes, you are a free man, but you have to still come with us to the hospital. Let us see what you can do for us in this matter please." He brought out two-page document, signed them, and gave it to them for them to also sign that I am actually being set free after nearly two years.

"Please, prepare his release papers in the next ten minutes. We need to go with him." They quickly went away to carry out the last order.

The hospital was a big one. It was situated somewhere closer to Poing, an outskirt of München. I was eager, much worried indeed to see Laura once again. I wasn't hoping to find her in the state the officials described to me. I was dreaming to see her in that old usual self with her usual laughter I used to know about her. My body was trebling all through; it was a feeling of fear and unexpected shock too. I wasn't sure if I could stand losing her to the storm of life, to the world of beyond, I tried not to think that way. I had always thought all this while, that maybe I shouldn't have brought her to Europe in the first place. I began to see my fault in all of this. I need to be blamed for all this, just me alone.

The chief nurse, Frau Kimbali, led us to the medical director's office. The passage we passed through was a sensitive part of the hospital. On usual circumstances, unauthorized people were never allowed into this vicinity, but for the men whom I came with, they were known to the hospital authorities. they had been coming there since their investigations started, and they are people in power, the high judge from Oberlandgericht in Berlin, the highest court of Germany. Now I understood why my release was so easy and fast. The court in Berlin overruled the decision of the lower court and set me free.

Mr. Donkaman, the chief medical director, was in his early fifties. From the fact I later put together about him, he was one of the best doctors in Bayern state. He had been acknowledged with many awards that have brought him so far in the medical field, including major accredited researches that gave him honors around the world. His judgment over a patient in most cases was the final result. We sat around a large table in his office.

"We have carried out major tests on these three patients. The results came back good, and they are medically okay, but yet they are not getting better despite all medications. This is beyond medical explanation now. They are fading out gradually," the doctor said as he sat up from his chair. "Their flesh is getting rotten like a spoiled banana, accompanied with a terrible odor. They are isolated from other patients. We thought it is a skin cancer, but tests came back negative, so it is not skin cancer. I am beginning to see their case outside of medical explanation, and we need external help if they are to survive." The curly haired man stared at him.

"But we can't give up on them yet. We must do all we can to save life," he said. "No, of course, I have requested for the presence of another practitioner in Scientology, a study of spiritual matters from Augsburg. We hope to have him here by tomorrow morning to examine them more closely and advice outside of medicine. We hope we can find a direction from there." "That's good news," the man with the spectacles said. "But, however, one of them would not stop calling the name, Paul all the time. Who is this Paul? Perhaps bringing this person to her could do something positive and help save the lives of others." The two men pointed at me. "This is the gentleman called Paul. We just got him out of the prison to come with us because one of the patients wants to see him." "That's good. What are we waiting for?" Kimbali said. He walked toward the door to lead the way to the ward; meanwhile we walked behind him in silence. We stopped to put on a white overall jacket, cover our nose, and wash our hands with a sanitizer before walking into the room.

I placed my hands on my mouth in a wondrous surprise. No medical equipment was fixed on her to indicate further treatment. I think they had just left her to die. I could not imagine what kind of illness was this; she was in a bad shape to put it mildly. The three men stood by the doorway, and by the instruction of Kimbali, I walked closer to her. She was in too much pain to notice my presence. The effect of the pain had been so much on her. With every second, she screamed out slowly with some trace of tears rolling down her face. I noticed how much she tried to endure the pains that were coming out of her body.

I turned around the bed and made myself visible to her sight. Although she was very weak, she managed to take a glance at me, and I could see she wanted to speak something to me, but the pains were unbearable. At the same time, she was in tears. I don't know if it was from the pain or guilt and reservation of regrets. How could we have chosen a destiny like this? I have always wanted to be a great guy, with a great accomplishment some day. We both had a dream of becoming engineers, to work in the same firm, a company of our own, and to do everything possible to bring our world into a life of great fulfillment, and to have a beautiful family. But I guess it's all over now.

I could not help it. Despite how terrible and disgusting she looked, tears would not stop gushing down my face like a little baby. I took the courage to go closer to her and held her by hand. "Baby," I said while holding her hand, "all will be okay with you. I am here for you, and I have forgiven you of everything already. I just pray that you will get better. I still love you, okay? And I will always love you like I never did before for the rest of my life." She shook her head continuously trying to say to me no, and it was not possible again. "Why?" I looked at her face.

"I am leaving you, Paul. I am passing on to the silent world where I now belong," she said with a very weak voice.

"No, you are going nowhere, my love," I said still holding her hand. "I am no longer angry with you." I was beginning to feel some vibration all over me. My body became cold suddenly, not knowing what to do at this moment. "We promised each other. We promised each other, Laura, never to leave each other and not this way." "But I disappointed you, Paul. I let you down. I fell for lies. They deceived me. I listened to them, and they made me to break my promise to you. I am sorry, so sorry. I allowed them to break my joy. The purpose I am meant to live for is gone. Now, I am paying a price that is too heavy for me." She stopped and went on crying. "I have forgiven you, my love. From the bottom of my heart, I have done that. I would not have agreed to come here if I have not forgiven you. We are not perfect. We are only humans. This is why you must stay with me. You have to fight for your life."

"I wish is that simple to do. I wish it is so easy. The Onigba spirits are real. Please tell others in our town not to make or repeat my mistakes. They are real. They have been coming to take my blood each time. I see them always, Paul. I should have listened to the voice of wisdom the Olu passed on to me when I was about to leave the town to join you. Oh, Paul, I wish I can turn back the hand of clock. Life has not been fair to me and my family. Please tell my mother to take heart. Ask her to forgive me for the pains I have caused her. I have not brought her joy. I have not given her grandchildren as I promised her. I have made her labor on me to come to nothing. Please ask her to forgive me so I can rest in peace on the other side . . ." Suddenly, she screamed at the top of her voice, "Look at them again. They are coming. Oh my God, please, Paul, help me . . ." She could not stop shouting. I looked but I could not see anything around her or touch her apart from me holding her hand. She continued to scream tirelessly as I presumed something most terrible was happening to her in a different world.

I could not see it or feel it, but from her cry of agony, I knew the gods were tormenting her. She was like going insane from her pains, a torture of her body and soul. It was unbearable to watch, and I cannot do anything to help her. I could no longer withstand her restlessness that Dr. Kimbali and three other male nurses rushed in to help pin her down to the bed. Just in less than four minutes of her total discomfort, she regained herself again, but this time, more weak and uncertain of what the next minutes hold for her.

The two gentlemen from the justice department were still not moving beyond the entrance door. They were looking at the unfolding drama from a distance. It was obvious there was a battle going on between the forces of evil and the power of God. From my religious belief, death was a transformation from one realm of life to the next life, from a living soul to join the spirit world. It does not mean the evil has won by causing a soul to die; it only happens by the commandment of the most high God. So, my God is always right in whatever he chooses to do and what he allows to happen in our lives.

The door went open. A young female nurse in her early twenties walked in. She was not looking bright whatsoever. She walked to the doctor and whispered in his ear. His face went sour at once. He hurriedly left the room with the four nurses who came to help to calm Laura again. It seemed there was another emergency that needed the doctor's attention.

It was bad news, nothing to jubilate about. Kerstin and Rachel had just passed away few moments ago. All effort to save them had failed, and they have given up the ghost. It was a sad period for everyone, especially for the doctors and the scientists who had been invited to find out the cause of this sickness that had defied all medical knowledge. It was a darkest moment of history in my life. I went to see their bodies in the room where both of them were kept, so it was true. I quickly went back to see Laura in her room. She was dosing in and out of sleep, so when I returned, I took a stool and sat close to her bed, looking deeply into her once beautiful eyes. I could not help becoming extra worried and fearful of what will become my fate on her. "I don't want it to happen!" I said quietly to myself.

I stood up and sat closer again by the edge of her bed. I touched her face, and she opened her eyes. "My love, Paul," she voiced in her usual weak, tired voice, "it is time to leave you alone. They ask me to say my last wishes."

"No, no, no," I cried aloud, "please don't leave me, Laura. My whole life will become empty without you, not after all I have endured in the name of love. I have seen and endured the pains in love. I need to be compensated through your stay. Please, your life must not be taken for the pains of love I have endured. Please, my beloved, don't do this to me."

My voice went cracking as if my throat was filling up with tears, and I was choking. "Let us celebrate life together. Please don't leave me."

"Promise me, Paul, I want you to move on, get another woman to give you the joy you truly deserved, love her, and marry her. But please don't forget me. I will be somewhere praying for you, and I will always talk to you in your dreams. Don't worry. Don't worry, my love." She suddenly screamed in total pain and blood began to gush out of her mouth.

I ran out of the room. "Someone help, please, doctor, nurses, please come and help me. We are losing her."

Doctors and nurses all ran into her room. Laura had fallen from her bed to the floor, lying lifeless. I was scared to come closer to her again. The doctor bent over her and tested if she was still alive, but there was no response from her. Laura is dead.

This is the story of my life, the end of an era, a sacrifice of love that ends up in sadness. Although she wished me to move on with life, I still don't know if it can be so easy to move on any longer. She is part of me, a woman that meant so dearly to my heart. We shared many secrets and unfolded situations together. Never can I forget her, a woman of my own soul.

END.

If Love Speaks

A spell, living beyond the imagination of man. A glorious fool that makes a difference in all stages of life.

A connection of truth that leads to all sides of human existence and reality.

Yesterday was the portrait of time, today, a circle of divine which identifies the hook.

A certainty and uncertainty of motion that rules all worlds, deep above the phrase of the living. Without it, there is no existence, and with it around, there is the beginning and the end of uncertainty.

It is a connection from the world of *mantle*, people of patience and sacrifice for what they cannot see.

A transformation of soul, while living in the world of reality which identifies the words in the purest form.
If only love speaks to man, natures would be of confusion, mind would emulate the silent world.

It is the beauty of the game, spider in a web of tears, deep in the image of time, master of them all.